THE BOOK

Machiavelli set out to write a practical guide to power. He chose as his model one of the most hated despots of the Renaissance—Cesare Borgia.

THE AUTHOR

Machiavelli was Borgia's enemy. Did he write *THE PRINCE* to praise this man to whom religion and ethics were mere stumbling blocks in the way of the shrewd politician? Or did he write it to damn him by means of bitter satire?

THE ACCLAIM

Spinoza and Rousseau insisted that *THE PRINCE* was a satire. Others portray Machiavelli as a ruthless and unprincipled cynic. Whatever his motives, *THE PRINCE* remains one of the preeminent works in the history of political literature— perhaps the most influential ever written.

P9-BBP-548

POCKET

Niccolo Machiavelli

The Prince

PUBLISHED BY POCKET BOOKS

**POCKET BOOKS, a Simon & Schuster division of
GULF & WESTERN CORPORATION
1230 Avenue of the Americas, New York, N.Y. 10020**

Introduction copyright © 1963 by Lester G. Crocker

ISBN: 0-671-82657-3

First Pocket Books printing August, 1963

19   18   17   16   15   14   13   12   11

Trademarks registered in the United States and other countries.

Printed in the U.S.A.

❦ CONTENTS ❧

v

Contents

Contents

৺§ INTRODUCTION ৡ৯

There is no list of "great books," or of "books that have most influenced men's minds," on which Machiavelli's *The Prince* does not appear. *The Prince* marks an important step in the history of western man: a step toward the modern world, with its complexities and conflicts; a step toward the nakedness of modern man, deprived of the shields of illusion. Because it says so much that is true and deeply significant, because of its enduring influence, and because it is written in the most pure and vigorous prose, *The Prince* is, quite simply, one of the great books of our heritage. Perhaps it is not too much to say that it is the most crucial work in the history of political literature, even when compared to Plato's *Republic,* Locke's *Treatises,* Rousseau's *Social Contract,* and *The Federalist Papers,* and *The Communist Manifesto.* This is a matter of personal judgment; but it certainly belongs, pre-eminently, in their company.

The books that have most deeply influenced the minds of men are quite often—perhaps most often—those whose interpretation is not too clear and unambiguous. Men of opposing opinions have been able to draw upon them, and they have been susceptible to renewed interpretation by different generations, according to the general attitudes and needs of each. Consequently, there is often lively controversy about the meaning and intent of such books—as we see in the case of *Hamlet, Don Quixote,* or the *Social*

Contract. This is also true of *The Prince.* To the seventeenth century, Machiavelli was a diabolical exponent of *Realpolitik;* to the patriots of the nineteenth century *Risorgimento,* he was a great patriot; to the Communists, he is an opponent of aristocracy and reaction. And perhaps, to a certain extent, Machiavelli strove for ambiguity in his writing. However, before we discuss the meaning of *The Prince,* we must look into the life of its author, for it is surely relevant to his work.

Niccolò Machiavelli was born on May 3, 1469, in the city and republic of Florence. His family had a rather distinguished history of patriotic service to the republic, and two centuries earlier had sided with the Guelphs—upholders of the independence of the city-states and allies of the papacy—against the Ghibellines, who were supporters of the Emperor, ruler of the Holy Roman Empire. A great granduncle, Girolamo, had undergone torture, exile and death in defense of the city's liberties. The generation into which Niccolò was born, however, was in modest financial circumstances and of undistinguished position. His father, Bernardo, was nonetheless conscious of his heritage. In addition to giving his son a good grounding in the Latin classics, he instilled in him a devotion to republican principles. There was a small library at home, and we are told that the copy of Livy had to be rebound by the time Niccolò was seventeen. He knew the ancient historians well, then. He read Italian literature, and studied music, too. But his education—in the narrow, as well as the broad sense of the word—was to be a continuous one. Although much influenced by a friend, the humanist Adriani, his own bent was eminently practical. Like Bacon, he sought knowledge not as an ornament, but for its uses.

Even in an early letter, his natural inclination reveals itself in his attitude toward Savonarola who, after having seized control upon the expulsion of the Medici, was approaching the disastrous ending that was to overtake him four years later. Machiavelli does not believe in the sincerity of Savonarola's messianic, puritanical mysticism. He sees only the drive for power and its mechanisms. An infidel himself, he considers religion only as a political fact —just as Hobbes, Montesquieu, Rousseau and later theorists were to do. What was clear to him was that Savonarola's sermons and prophecies had unified his party and divided his enemies. This was a political fact.

In the 1480's, the Florentines began to realize how their ancient freedoms had been gradually gnawed away by the patient craftiness of the Medici family. In 1494, they rebelled, and Piero de' Medici was expelled from the city. In that year, Machiavelli entered the government service. Before long, he had become secretary of the Signoria, chancellor of the second chancery, and secretary to the Ten of War. He served the republic with outstanding zeal and skill, and was commended for these qualities. He might also have been praised for his scrupulous honesty. He was later made paymaster general of the army. When he left the public service, however, he was—like Sancho Panza leaving his government—as naked as when he entered it.

During his fourteen years of service, Machiavelli's penetrating eye and analytical mind were absorbing the realities of human motivation and of political power. Most valuable to his understanding of these matters were his missions to other Italian governments, and to the court of France, missions which were confided to him after the war with

Pisa had been renewed. He also witnessed the rebellion of Arezzo, headed by one of Cesare Borgia's *condottieri,* Vitellozzo Vitelli, to whom he was sent in 1502. He was impressed by Borgia's ambition to create a strong, unified state in central Italy, and gave much thought to such urgent problems as the role of France in Italian politics and other current power relationships. Machiavelli's letters to his friend, Vettori, confirm the admiration we see in *The Prince* for Borgia's audacious yet calculated decisiveness, for his skillful use of cruelty and fraud, his reliance on native troops and his administration of conquered provinces. He saw in these tactics a model for dealing with false friends and unsure allies. Borgia, however, was to come to a sorry and contemptible end. Whether the Cesare Borgia Machiavelli wrote about in *The Prince* is a parody of this real Borgia or an ideal image projected from his earlier view is a point in dispute.

In 1502, Machiavelli married Marietta Corsini; they seem to have had a happy home, despite his frequent infidelities. Meanwhile, he had also become involved in the organization of a Florentine militia, one of his pet projects; in this task he assisted Piero Soderini, gonfalonier of the city. Wise though he was in planning, Machiavelli apparently showed less wisdom in appointing Don Micheletto, one of Borgia's killers, as commander; for mere ruthlessness was not what was needed to instill spirit and civic pride in the troops.

Amid these and other activities, Machiavelli found distraction in writing. In 1504 he composed a poem, *Annals of Italy,* and a comedy. His knowledge of political affairs was further broadened by a mission to the court of Emperor Maximilian; traveling in many parts of Switzerland

and the Empire, he studied German politics and national character, reporting on these subjects to his government. A mission to Louis XII, in 1510, produced another report, on "Affairs in France," which is also distinguished by its analytical clarity.

The year before, Pisa had at last surrendered, and to Machiavelli went much of the credit. But the good fortune was not to last. Spain and France were both casting covetous eyes on the weakening government of Florence, and the Medici were covertly planning a comeback. The French were driven out of northern Italy by the forces of the warrior-pope, Julius II, in May of 1512; but Cardinal Giovanni de' Medici led a Spanish army into Tuscany and put Prato to the sack. Panic coursed through the city of Florence. Machiavelli's militia had failed. The government of his friend and protector, Soderini, was turned out, and the Medici, headed by Giuliano, were welcomed back by a fawning citizenry. Despite all this, and despite the knowledge that he had made many enemies, Machiavelli hoped to swing over with the others and hold on to some of his offices. But his overtures to the Medici were spurned, and he was sent into exile in November of that year. Only a few months later, he was arrested for involvement in a conspiracy to overthrow the government, his name having been found on a list in the possession of one of the conspirators. He confessed nothing, despite the unusually prolonged torture of six turns on the rack. The lesson learned, he retired to his farm, shutting the doors on his political career.

Books and writing had been his recreation, not his occupation. He found his new inactivity tedious and irritating. But he did write, seeking recreation now in dissipation and debauchery. With the ambiguity that characterizes his life, his character and his writings, he could frequent with equal pleasure high-minded immortals in his study or gross and vulgar companions in his roistering.

His great effort was on the magnificent *Discourses on the First Ten Books of Livy* (usually referred to as the *Discorsi*). After writing his commentary on the first books, he realized that their completion might be delayed too long to help him regain the favor of the Medici. For this reason, he interrupted that project to compose a brief and pungent summary of his thinking and his experience. This work, *The Prince,* took him only a few months to write, in the year 1513. For some reason, he kept the manuscript in his desk, instead of sending it to Giuliano de' Medici, to whom he was planning to dedicate it. Giuliano died in 1516. He then dedicated it to Lorenzo, and sent it to him. Lorenzo never acknowledged it, and Machiavelli, it is interesting to note, never published his book. Although there was some covert circulation of manuscripts, *The Prince* did not reach the presses until 1532, five years after his death.

Meanwhile, Machiavelli from time to time read his *Discorsi* to friends, and was not reluctant to stir up their republican sentiments. In 1519 Giovanni de' Medici, now Pope Leo X, and his cousin, Cardinal Giulio, did turn to Machiavelli, but only for advice about the problems of governing the republic. Machiavelli's response was a treatise urging a free state system. In 1520, he published an *Art of War* which called for national armies and deprecated the value of artillery in favor of infantry; and also the life of Castruccio Castracani, which was part biography, part romance. Castruccio was really a medieval freebooter who had succeeded, by courage, daring and skill (a combination Machiavelli calls *virtù*) in gaining possession of several Tuscan cities. If we compare this portrait with that of Cesare Borgia in *The Prince,* it is possible to think of both as idealized models. Machiavelli was also commissioned, by Giulio, to write a history of Florence, for which he was to receive an annual allowance of one hundred florins—a most welcome reinforcement to the impoverished writer. The *Istorie fiorentine,* as he called the work, is not straight history, but a critical view based on his general political principles—one which deduces lessons for the future. To these works we must add his great play, *Mandragola* (1524), a comedy in the tradition of Boccaccio. Ribald and biting, it paints the moral corruption of the time—in a way of all times, for in it, men are divided into two classes: the stupid dupes and the clever scoundrels who victimize them. The story tells how an adventurer, lusting for the virtuous wife of a townsman, succeeds (thanks to his own cleverness) in spending a night with her with the husband's consent, the help of the mother, who wants to see her daughter pregnant, and, above all, the hypocritical knavery of an avaricious confessor. The results are satisfactory to all. In the deeper view, the underlying philosophy of *Mandragola* is also that of *The Prince*—trickery and daring governing men according to the will of the one who has superior *virtù.* Such is the law of life.

In 1526 Machiavelli was sent on a number of missions by Giulio de' Medici, now Pope Clement VII, under the direction of his fellow political philosopher, Francesco Guicciardini, with whom he became closely associated. He seemed on the verge of a new diplomatic career. But in June of 1527, just when the Medici were again driven from Florence, and when he might have returned to the service of the republic, he fell ill of a digestive ailment. He took some medicine, and this, according to a letter written by his son, killed him, on the 21st day of that month.

There is much that can be said in criticism of Machiavelli's life and character. His conversation was often sarcastic. He was unscrupulous, and boasted that he was such an accomplished liar that he could make people think he was lying when he said the truth. His correspondence is cynical and often astoundingly coarse. He idealized the successful Cesare Borgia and turned against him when he failed. His great qualities were those of his mind, and his devotion to the welfare of his city and country. His faults reflect the neo-pagan spirit of his age. As for his attitude toward human nature, which has been called crude and cynical, the history of our own time has shown it to contain bitter truths we should have done well to face with the candor and courage that he showed.

It is important to realize that *The Prince,* one of the most strikingly original of books, grew, like its author, out of its age and its people. Such works as *The Prince, Don Quixote* and *Pilgrim's Progress* spring from native roots, during periods of disorganization, change and critical self-examination. Florence was the Athens of Renaissance Italy, and its citizens, like those of the ancient city, were involved in politics as well as in letters and arts. Republics both, they were in actuality ruled by superior men, with the tacit or voiced consent of the citizenry. But Florence, far worse than Athens, was agitated by factions, and had been ever since the strife between Guelphs and Ghibellines, with class conflicts and family rivalries succeed-

ing one another. Already Dante, in the sixth canto of
Purgatory, had cursed out the turbulent spirit of the Italians through the tongue of the poet, Sordello:

"Hostel of woe, ah, servile Italy,
  Vessel unpiloted in a great storm,
  No Lady of Provinces, but harlotry. . . .
  While now in civil tumult are distraught
  Thy living citizens—at daggers drawn
  Those whom one wall encloses, and one moat."

After a succession of governments, established and disestablished to the tune of conspiracies, treacheries, murders and banishments—despite the fact that most were led by responsible and patriotic aristocrats—the firm and wise rule of Cosimo de' Medici had come as a welcome interval. But even he had been done in by the intrigues of factions: banished, a year after coming to power, with the howling mob ready to lynch him—only to return triumphant a year later. The same situation prevailed throughout Italy, but it was worst in Florence. We must note the participation of Church dignitaries, including the popes, in these acts. This points to their significant characteristic—their existence outside the realm of moral evaluation. Enterprise was legitimate; it was only failing or succeeding that was subject to judgment, that brought blame and derision, praise and adulation, upon the actors in the drama. In a word, successful treachery and murder were accepted instruments of politics.

This was the milieu in which Machiavelli lived, and we cannot without blindness or hypocrisy expect him to have freed himself entirely from it and to have risen wholly above it. If his study of history revealed to him some exceptional examples of human nobility, it also confirmed the universality of a ruthless power struggle in which the real and ultimate criterion of judgment was success or failure. That is why the subject of *The Prince* is the *means* to success and failure. These facts enable us to realize how inappropriate it is to condemn Machiavelli as vicious and satanic, or to refuse to take him at face value on the grounds that a man so intelligent and high-minded as he could not have been serious.

This brings us to the principal conflict of interpretations. Alberico Gentile, in the sixteenth century, and later Spinoza, Rousseau and Macaulay, all insisted that *The Prince* was a work of satire, with hidden meanings, whose intent was to warn the people about what they could expect from a prince's rule. "In pretending to give lessons to kings," writes Rousseau in the third book of the *Social Contract,* "he has given great lessons to peoples. Machiavelli's *Prince* is the book of republicans." According to Rousseau, Machiavelli was forced, by oppression, "to disguise his love of liberty . . . and the contrast between the maxims of *The Prince* and those of the *Discourses,* and of his *History of Florence,* proves that this deep politician has had up till now only superficial or corrupted readers." Rousseau's own statement, however, would tend to prove exactly the opposite of what he asserts. If Machiavelli did express his republican sentiments elsewhere, and in published writings, it could scarcely have been fear of oppression that prevented him from doing likewise in *The Prince.* The fact that it was *The Prince* which he did not dare or care to publish—the work which favored strong princes —might well indicate either that he no longer believed in its personal usefulness to him, or that he thought it prudent not to expose the ultimate radicalism of his thought to public view.

Recently, the interpretation of *The Prince* as satire has been powerfully revived. Certain historians point out that although much of that work is in perfect harmony with his thinking elsewhere, in other aspects, it is contradictory to his life and writings. Machiavelli, they say, could not have wanted a tyrant to rule the free people of Florence. He and his ancestors were devoted to the republic, which they had long served. In the *Discorsi,* he defended popular rule. He had a feeling for the public taste and reaction—but *The Prince* shocked and horrified its readers. If it was meant seriously, it was an artistic blunder, precisely because it shocks. It would have been insulting to Giuliano de' Medici, since it urges him to imitate the hated bastard son of a pope—Cesare Borgia—who had proven such a pitiable failure, and was obviously a perfect model for a satire. In addition, Giuliano was both gentle and lazy—scarcely the type to respond to Machiavelli's stirring call to violent action. And, in fact, he loathed the Borgia. Actually, then, *The Prince* was a satire of the many current books of advice to princes, for the Renaissance hated the tyrants Machiavelli feigned to admire. It was, in reality, a taunt and a challenge to the Medici, and a call to the Florentines to throw off the yoke. The Medici probably recognized this, but did not punish Machiavelli because that would have revealed their hand.

Many are not at all convinced by this circumstantial argument. A tyrant, they might argue, was ruling people who were not free when Machiavelli wrote his book, and he was concerned with actualities. If at times he defended popular rule, at other times he expressed a very contemptuous opinion of the people, inveighed against their insubordination and fickleness, and spoke of the "nauseous rule of the rabble." If he was devoted to the republic, he was bitterly disappointed by the behavior of the Florentines, by their disunity and utter lack of public spirit, by their refusal to heed his advice. It is useless to guess what motives he had in mind in dedicating his book to the ruler of Florence, and idle speculation to suggest how the latter reacted to it. If *The Prince* was intended as a satire, it was an artistic blunder. A satire, if good, also shocks; but what good is a satire which practically nobody takes to be a satire? Surely, *The Prince* is full of straightforward, face-value truths, expressed with an impressive cogency. This would make it a most peculiar hybrid, in which one would have to disentangle what is intended as satire—with great difficulty, moreover, since it is a work of singular coherence and relentless logic. It is doubtful whether literary critics would be willing to take most of its pages as satire. Finally, the prudence which Machiavelli showed in not publishing this work—and only this one of his works —during his lifetime can scarcely be taken as an indication that it was a satire, since he sent it to the very man whom (or whose family), it is claimed, he intended to satirize. If it was a satire, the sending of it was not an act of prudence; if it was not a satire, the withholding of the work may well be interpreted to mean that Machiavelli intended it quite seriously, but was worried, and had been cautioned, about possible reaction.

Machiavelli himself confirms his seriousness of purpose in a letter of December 10, 1513 to his friend, Vettori. His conversations with books, he states, had led him to write *The Prince,* "in which I delve as deeply as I can into reflections on this subject . . . and if any of my scribblings has ever pleased you, this one should not displease you; and to a prince, and above all to a new prince, it should be welcome." In the last analysis, the *Discorsi* and *The Prince* are essentially consonant, if we allow for the fact that one deals with a republic, the other with monarchies or absolute governments. It is true that in the former he expresses enthusiasm for popular government, but he indubitably believed it to be out of the question in the Italy of his time. The problem he faced was that of founding a state in a corrupt society, which lacked the private and public morality, and especially the civic devotion, that had made the Roman republic viable.

Arguments such as these are, on both sides, pure conjecture, and evidence can be thrust forward and countered with no end and to little purpose. Perhaps we can never know with certainty what Machiavelli intended. This would be important from the viewpoint of "local" history. In the broader view, however, of the intellectual and political history of the West, it is not very important. What matters is how *The Prince* has actually been read, and what its influence has been. And here the "satirical" interpretation is largely irrelevant. It is also true that Machiavelli's theories are not to be judged only by what he wrote in *The Prince*. They are complex, and the *Discorsi,* among other writings, must be given full consideration. But that again is a particular problem, for the *Discorsi* have had less influence. It is also quite possible to consider *The Prince* as part of a "negative phase" of pessimistic realism, which included a polemical movement against the humanists of the time, with their idealized states and perfect princes, against the theological moralism of certain medieval political doctrines, and against blind, uncourageous traditionalism. On such a view, the *Discorsi* would represent a "positive phase," one in which Machiavelli, thinking of the happier days of the Roman republic, expressed his longing for a social life worthier of mankind, and showed the conditions, difficult but not impossible, under which better times might again come into existence.

The important fact is that *The Prince* is a starting point for any study of Renaissance political thought or modern political thought. It is not that this, or any other work, is cut off from its heritage in the past. Elements of the theory of the omnipotent, secular state can be found in the Middle Ages; moreover, it took some years before Machiavelli's views (in conjunction with historical events) finally eliminated the idea that the state reflected and should reflect the law of God, coequally with the Church. But it was gradually (even if tacitly) recognized that Machiavelli's analysis, though it was loudly condemned as odious, was by and large a description of reality.

At the very time Machiavelli was writing, the dominant humanistic outlook in political theory was being carried to its highest point in the works of Erasmus (*The Education of a Christian Prince*, 1515) and of Sir Thomas More (*Utopia*, 1516). But the events and conditions in Italy, especially the social and economic crisis and the French invasion, added to a developing naturalism, had led to a decisive break with the Christian-humanistic-natural law tradition. The year 1494, when Charles VIII invaded Italy, marked the onset of a period of upheaval during which European states were to struggle for their unity and to affirm their power, with Italy one of the main arenas of struggle. The new thinking was swiftly brought to a focus, in a radical form, in *The Prince.* To be sure, the medieval natural law tradition persisted, gradually transformed by the Reformation, by the consequences of scientific naturalism and by an emphasis in some quarters on natural rights. But *The Prince* was on the main line of actual historical development. The following centuries were to witness the combat against feudalism, the creation of unitarian states, the struggle between them, and the manipulation of peoples. Machiavelli's many errors in judgment and in historical perspective, the very narrowness and poverty of his world view were, in his case, virtues. They led to a simplification, to a clarity of definition that gave his book its vitality. Not until our own time has the menace of the all-absorbing, all-controlling Leviathan become evident; thus, when in the eighteenth century Voltaire disagreed with Montesquieu about the need for intermediary powers, or when Rousseau conceived what we should have to call a proto-totalitarian state, they had no notion, even then, of its latent possibilities. In modern times, it has been the currents associated with civil liberties and the rights of man, rather than the Church, which have been the effective force opposing the Machiavellian view and limiting the power of the State.

The Prince owes its great historical impact to two crucial viewpoints which inform it. In the first place, it treats all matters relating to politics and human behavior in general as purely natural phenomena, capable of objective analysis and control. In the second place, following this consistent naturalism, it considers success in achieving one's goals, in the personal or interstate struggle for survival, to be the only real or meaningful criterion of acts. Both these basic ideas are developed throughout the book with a wealth of concrete examples and astute analytical reasoning. From fact, Machiavelli rises to general truth, and that he in turn applies to the situation at hand. *The Prince* is already a model of "scientific method."

Machiavelli sees history as an interplay between fortune and *virtù*. He believes that the will, courage and skill implied by the latter term can be dominant; fortune, he says, is like a woman "if you wish to master her, you must strike and beat her." Believing, then, that men's destiny lies largely in their own hands, his urgent desire is to promote *virtù* in his own country, and so to establish stable and successful government, ultimately to expel the foreigner and even to unite the country into one nation. His observations from recent events and from ancient history all point in the same direction. His viewpoint is always that of the ruler, and of the difficulties he faces in maintaining his power; this is the sole consideration.

Machiavelli examines these problems in every possible situation. He weighs the favorable factors in each case, and the dangerous ones, then goes on to analyze the means of maximizing the former and minimizing the latter. Moral considerations are excluded as simply irrelevant and extraneous, except where an evil reputation would become a political detriment. Thus he argues that it is useful to establish colonies by depriving some inhabitants of their homes and farms; they will be poor and despised, and so unable to do any harm, while the rest will be frightened about their own possessions. An opposing family must be completely wiped out. "Men must be either cozened or crushed," for society is a perpetual power struggle, a war even in peace. Louis XII was to blame, not for having tried to conquer Italy, but for the mistakes he made. The desire for conquest is *natural*. If the king was powerful enough to conquer successfully, he was right to do so. "A war," Machiavelli also notes cogently, "is never avoided, but is only deferred to one's own disadvantage." (However, it is obvious that this cannot be true for both sides.) The three ways of holding states accustomed to self-government are to ruin them, to reside in them, or to set up what we should call puppet governments. A free people will always rise up, when they can, and so destruction and dispersion are necessary in that case. Those rulers who come to power from the ranks can do so only by a juncture of will, skill and favorable circumstance. In their situation persuasion is useless; belief must be compelled and opposition ruthlessly crushed; only then can a new order of things be established. (This lesson has been well learned by the modern totalitarian countries.) In the seventh chapter, Machiavelli gives us a picture of the intrigues, deceits and barbarous cruelties of the Italian popes and princes. None of these touches any moral chord in him; they are just natural facts of power politics. He cites with apparent approval, and as a model for imitation, Borgia's murder of a henchman, whose fine work had greatly helped him, when his disappearance became politically expedient. (This lesson, too, has been learned by the totalitarians.) Later Machiavelli does condemn outrageous cruelty and inhumanity; but he takes the view that the perpetrator, when he succeeds, must be admired for his success. The criterion, ultimately, is the ruler's ability to maintain himself. And he tells rulers and would-be rulers how such deeds should be carried out, when they must. But where a ruler rises to power on the wings of popular favor, it is shrewdness that is called for, rather than violence. Delving into the various possibilities, Machiavelli concludes that the best policy is for him to make himself "the voice of the people," and so prevent the rise of rivals seeking to undercut him, or to cut his throat. If powerful allies must be used, there are ways of dealing with them, and of getting rid of them in time. When it comes to the ecclesiastic states, their power politics is discussed with obvious irony; they are considered as subject to all the rules of the game, with scarcely a nod to the Church's spiritual pretensions.

"I shall differ from the rules laid down by others," writes Machiavelli. "Reality" is his guide. "For the manner in which men live is so different from the way in which they ought to live, that he who leaves the common course for that which he ought to follow will find that it leads him to ruin rather than to safety." It is all right to be good, when it is helpful, or when necessity requires it, but it is folly to follow virtues which lead to ruin. Similarly with vices: those leading to ruin are to be avoided, those which are useful are to be adopted. In some instances, the reputation for a virtue, like mercy, is desirable, but the virtue itself is dangerous. Cruelty, by accomplishing the ends of peace and order, may be mercy. It is best to be both feared and loved, but since this feat is a difficult one, it is best to be feared. Why is this so? Because of human nature, replies Machiavelli, which is ever ungrateful, cowardly, fickle and selfish. Because men are essentially evil, the bonds of love and obligation do not withstand the force of self-interest. But fear of punishment is powerful. The prince must know men for what they are, selfish beings whose aggressiveness and acquisitiveness, bounded only by natural limits and by competition, would lead them to anarchy, unless government intervened. That is why a ruler, and government in general, concerned with basic issues of order and survival, are above ordinary moral rules. The safety of the state and the survival of the ruler and of his government are the supreme laws. The criterion, says Machiavelli again and again, is success: who gets the better of whom, who wins and who loses. To put it crudely—as he does—men must be animals, be like all else in nature, and not try to be human beings. The law of nature is force. "A prince should know how to employ the nature of man, and that of the beasts as well." Within the state, men can be made to "be good," that is, order can be preserved. But this can be accomplished only by force, deceit, the inculcation of habit, and the inhibitory effect of religion (but not including Christianity, which makes men otherworldly, uncivic, and unmanly).

The ruler, then, must be a lion and a fox. He will "feel out" just how far he can go. Knowing human nature, he will not molest his subjects' women or confiscate their property: "for men will sooner forget the death of their fathers than the loss of their patrimony." He will break his pledges when it is in his interest to do so. The justification is that men will not keep faith with you. Good faith would be nice, if it were practical; but trickery and deceit are the ways to achieve and to maintain power. (It is clear that Machiavelli sees society as a constant, if undeclared, state of war: "men will always prove naturally bad, unless some necessity constrains them to be good.") But when the ruler breaks his pledge, he must do it right, and find "legitimate reasons" with which "to color his want of good faith." In a word, he must not only be powerful and ruthless, but "a great hypocrite and dissembler." Hypocrisy is established as the highest of political virtues. The world, says Machiavelli, is full of dupes, implying that one must be either exploiter or victim, shearer or shorn. And means are always both justifiable and honored, if they eventuate in success. Or, as he puts it in *The Life of Castruccio Castracani,* "men should attempt everything and not be dismayed by anything; for God loves strong men, since we see that he always punishes the weak through the strong."

In all this adroit analysis and advice, Machiavelli apparently felt that he was only putting into concrete form what men had been doing for ages, and what they were doing still, without arousing marked disapproval; often, in fact, with praise and admiration. He put into rational formulations what were the real and effective rules and gambits of power politics. But the importance of *The Prince* lies in the fact that it is something more than a technical manual of statecraft. On reading it, we know that we are reading a great work, one which deals with fundamentals of government, of political relations, of human nature, of man as a political being. Its chiseled sentences, classical in purity, vivid and plastic, stamp out propositions that go to the heart of human social life and its problems. Machiavelli knew well that this is a hard and bitter world, and he was not one to pull down the blinds.

In our own age, the broader philosophical significance of *The Prince* seems more important than the narrower political program. The basic position is clear and unmistakable. Politics and morals are divorced. Each of the two has its own ends, each its own means. They are not reconcilable. There is no middle position of compromise. One is either a politician or a moralist, a ruler or a Christian. In the government of men and the dealings between governments, Christian morality is replaced by another set of values. Perhaps one may go so far as to assert a "political morality," set off against ethical morality—but Machiavelli does not even make such a claim. He is far from oblivious to ethical claims, but he considers that morality is itself an instrument of government, inasmuch as moral corruption in a people makes good government impossible. The civic virtues must be cultivated, and so morality is one of the political forces which must be reckoned with, and utilized—as religion is another. It is simply, then, that in *The Prince* all problems of justice are resolved into problems of mechanics. Society is a system of forces in which the loser is always wrong. Fact constitutes right. Since law without effective force is, due to the nature of man, only myth, force alone is real. We know today, more clearly than ever, what fruits such a doctrine can bear. When the state may demand of those who rule the sacrifice of every principle and the renunciation of every sentiment, then we are on the road to those philosophies (such as Rousseau's, Herder's, or the totalitarians') which conceive of the state not only as above morality, but as the highest moral entity. Yet, from another view, it is not for us to condemn Machiavelli, but only to weigh whether what he says is true. To condemn him, we must go outside of his frame of reference, and judge him by what we think ought to be; whereas his purpose is only to tell us what has been and what is—not even to tell us what can be.

The Prince stands at an important crossroads in the

history of western culture. The fundamental intellectual unity of the Middle Ages was dissolving, as a result of the breaking of all kinds of closed horizons. Certainties were shaken, as the baroque mind became obsessed with its favorite dichotomy, that of appearance and reality. This fissure threads its way across the pages of *The Prince,* and we see it best when Machiavelli advises that it is wiser to *seem* to have qualities than to have them, for men know only appearance. It was also a time when the optimism of the humanistic outlook was to be ever more swiftly transmuted into pessimism. The beautiful and comforting hierarchical pattern of the universe, with God's omniscient eye at its summit, was crumbling under the weight of a new cosmology and a rising naturalism. Many old ideas, of basic importance, could no longer be held with sincerity. Man did not seem to be made in the image of God, but to be closer to the beasts. The State was not the guardian of any universal, God-given or natural law, but a human device inseparable from human needs and passions, based on force, not right.

These ideas, which Machiavelli was the first to express with power and with candor, were as truly revolutionary as any ideas have ever been. They signal a revolt against the Christian-humanistic tradition of a divinely established congruence between real and ideal, against the tradition of a law of reason and limit, inscribed in the universe, and relevant to human life. Machiavelli either ignores or scorns the belief that above the prince's personal and political aims stand the laws of God, guiding him down the best path for human welfare.

These ideas usher in the modern world, and bury the medieval. Their repercussions echoed throughout Europe, in the essays of Montaigne, in the *First Anniversary* of Donne, and above all, in the tragedies of Shakespeare, where the splitting of appearance and reality, and the confrontation with man's true nature and destiny take on their widest and deepest dimensions. Among the truths to which they lead—and this is the one in which Machiavelli was most interested—is the necessity for man, with his dual nature, to live simultaneously in two worlds, the political and the moral. Each has its claims on us. Each is of a nature apparently so different, that we have not yet succeeded, and perhaps never can succeed, in fusing them. We must live as men, uneasily, with one foot in each world, aspiring to those very values which we ourselves deny and destroy.

LESTER G. CROCKER
Western Reserve University

ABOUT THE EDITOR
Lester G. Crocker, Ph.D., an eminent American authority on Romance literature, has taught at a number of distinguished institutions, among which are the University of California, Sweet Briar College, Goucher College, the Institute for Advanced Study, the University of London and Western Reserve University. He has been both a Fulbright Research Scholar and a Guggenheim Fellow. He has written and edited a number of books, including three on Diderot. At this time, Dr. Crocker is Dean of Humanities, Case Western Reserve University.

✧ BIBLIOGRAPHY ❧

The standard edition of Machiavelli's works in the original Italian is *Tutte le opere storiche e letterarie di Niccolò Machiavelli,* ed. Guido Mazzoni and Mario Casella (Firenze, 1929). The best biographies in English are Jeffrey Pulver, *Machiavelli: The Man, His Work & His Times* (London, 1937); and D. E. Muir, *Machiavelli and His Times* (London, 1936). For the historical background see L. A. Burd, "Florence (II): Machiavelli," in *The Cambridge Modern History,* Vol. I (New York, 1934): 190-218; Ferdinand Schevill, *History of Florence from the Founding of the City through the Renaissance* (New York, 1936); Jacob Burckhardt, *The Civilization of the Renaissance in Italy* (Oxford, 1945), Pt. I, "The State as a Work of Art"; Ralph Roeder, *The Man of the Renaissance* (New York, 1933).

For the tradition of political thought behind Machiavelli's work, see Allan H. Gilbert, *Machiavelli's "Prince" and Its Forerunners* (Durham, North Carolina, 1938); and Felix Gilbert, "The Humanist Concept of the Prince and *The Prince* of Machiavelli," *The Journal of Modern History,* XI (1939): 449-483, and the same author's "Political Thought of the Renaissance and Reformation," *The Huntington Library Quarterly,* IV (1941): 443-468.

For Machiavelli's place in Elizabethan literature, see Mario Praz, *Machiavelli and the Elizabethans,* Annual Italian Lecture, Proceedings of the British Academy (London, 1928), and Wyndham Lewis, *The Lion and the Fox* (London, 1927): 59-114.

Two recent novels that have been written around Machiavelli and his time are Maurice Samuel, *Web of Lucifer* (New York, 1947), and W. Somerset Maugham, *Then and Now* (New York, 1946).

Niccolò Machiavelli

TO THE

Magnificent Lorenzo, son of Piero de' Medici

Those who desire to win the favor of princes generally endeavor to do so by offering them those things which they themselves prize most, or such as they observe the prince to delight in most. Thence it is that princes have very often presented to them horses, arms, cloth of gold, precious stones, and similar ornaments worthy of their greatness. Wishing now myself to offer to your Magnificence some proof of my devotion, I have found nothing among all I possess that I hold more dear or esteem more highly than the knowledge of the actions of great men, which I have acquired by long experience of modern affairs, and a continued study of ancient history.

These I have meditated upon for a long time, and examined with great care and diligence; and having now written them out in a small volume, I send this to your Magnificence. And although I judge this work unworthy of you, yet I trust that your kindness of heart may induce you to accept it, considering that I cannot offer you anything better than the means of understanding in the briefest time all that which I have learned by so many years of study, and with so much trouble and danger to myself.

I have not set off this little work with pompous phrases, nor filled it with high-sounding and magnificent words, nor with any other allurements or extrinsic embellishments with which many are wont to write and adorn their works; for I wished that mine should derive credit only from the truth of the matter, and that the importance of the subject should make it acceptable.

And I hope it may not be accounted presumption if a man of lowly and humble station ventures to discuss and direct the conduct of princes; for as those who wish to delineate countries place themselves low in the plain to observe the form and character of mountains and high places, and for the purpose of studying the nature of the low country place themselves high upon an eminence, so one must be a prince to know well the character of the people, and to understand well the nature of a prince one must be of the people.

May your Magnificence then accept this little gift in the same spirit in which I send it; and if you will read and consider it well, you will recognize in it my desire that you may attain that greatness which fortune and your great qualities promise. And if your Magnificence will turn your eyes from the summit of your greatness toward those low places, you will know how undeservedly I have to bear the great and continued malice of fortune.

The Prince

CHAPTER I

*HOW MANY KINDS OF PRINCIPALITIES
THERE ARE, AND IN WHAT MANNER
THEY ARE ACQUIRED*

All states and governments that have had, and have at present, dominion over men, have been and are either republics or principalities.

The principalities are either hereditary or they are new. Hereditary principalities are those where the government has been for a long time in the family of the prince. New principalities are either entirely new, as was Milan to Francesco Sforza, or they are like appurtenances annexed to the hereditary state of the prince who acquires them, as the kingdom of Naples is to that of Spain.

States thus acquired have been accustomed either to live under a prince, or to exist as free states; and they are acquired either by the arms of others, or by the conqueror's own, or by fortune or personal courage and talents.

CHAPTER II

OF HEREDITARY PRINCIPALITIES

I will not discuss here the subject of republics, having treated of them at length elsewhere,[1] but will confine myself only to principalities; and following the above indicated order of distinctions, I will proceed to discuss how states of this kind should be governed and maintained. I say, then, that hereditary states, accustomed to the line of their prince, are maintained with much less difficulty than new states. For it is enough merely that the prince do not transcend the order of things established by his predecessors, and then to accommodate himself to events as they occur. So that if such a prince has but ordinary sagacity, he will always maintain himself in his state, unless some extraordinary force should deprive him of it. And even in such a case he will recover it, whenever the occupant meets with any reverses. We have in Italy, for instance, the Duke of Ferrara, who could not have resisted the assaults of the Venetians in 1484, nor those of Pope Julius II in 1510, but for the fact that his family had for a great length of time held the sovereignty of that dominion. For the natural prince has less cause and less necessity for irritating his subjects, whence it is reasonable that he should be more beloved. And unless extraordinary vices should cause him to be hated, he will naturally have

---

[1] In the essay on Livy in the *Discourses*.

the affection of his people. For in the antiquity and continuity of dominion the memory of innovations, and their causes, are effaced; for each change and alteration always prepares the way and facilitates the next.

CHAPTER III

OF MIXED PRINCIPALITIES

But it is in a new principality that difficulties present themselves. In the first place, if it be not entirely new, but composed of different parts, which when taken all together may as it were be called mixed, its mutations arise in the beginning from a natural difficulty, which is inherent in all new principalities, because men change their rulers gladly, in the belief that they will better themselves by the change. It is this belief that makes them take up arms against the reigning prince; but in this they deceive themselves, for they find afterward from experience that they have only made their condition worse. This is the inevitable consequence of another natural and ordinary necessity, which ever obliges a new prince to vex his people with the maintenance of an armed force, and by an infinite number of other wrongs that follow in the train of new conquests. Thus the new prince finds that he has for enemies all those whom he has injured by seizing that principality; and at the same time he cannot preserve as friends even those who have aided him in obtaining possession, because he cannot satisfy their expectations, nor can he employ strong measures against them, being under obligation to them. For however strong a new prince may be in troops, yet will he always have need of the good will of the inhabitants, if he wishes to enter into firm possession of the country.

It was for these reasons that Louis XII, King of France, having suddenly made himself master of Milan, lost it as quickly, Lodovico Sforza's own troops alone having sufficed to wrest it from him the first time. For the very people who had opened the gates to Louis XII, finding themselves deceived in their expectations of immediate as well as prospective advantages, soon became disgusted with the burdens imposed by the new prince.

It is very true that, having recovered such revolted provinces, it is easier to keep them in subjection; for the prince will avail himself of the occasion of the rebellion to secure himself, with less consideration for the people, by punishing the guilty, watching the suspected, and strengthening himself at all the weak points of the province. Thus a mere demonstration on the frontier by Lodovico Sforza lost Milan to the French the first time; but to make them lose it a second time required the whole world to be against them, and that their armies should be dispersed and driven out of Italy; which resulted from the reasons which I have explained above. Nevertheless, France lost Milan both the first and the second time.

The general causes of the first loss have been sufficiently explained; but it remains to be seen now what occasioned the loss of Milan to France the second time, and to point out the remedies which the King had at his command, and which might be employed by any other prince under similar circumstances to maintain himself in a conquered province, but which King Louis XII failed to employ.

I will say then, first, that the states which a prince acquires and annexes to his own dominions are either in the same country, speaking the same language, or they are not. When they are, it is very easy to hold them, especially if they have not been accustomed to govern themselves; for in that case it suffices to extinguish the line of the prince who, till then, has ruled over them, but otherwise to maintain their old institutions. There being no difference in their manners and customs, the inhabitants will submit quietly, as we have seen in the case of Burgundy, Brittany, Gascony, and Normandy, which provinces have remained so long united to France. For although there are some differences of language, yet their customs are similar, and therefore they were easily reconciled to each other. Hence, in order to retain a newly acquired state, regard must be had to two things: one, that the line of the ancient sovereign be entirely extinguished; and the other, that the laws be not changed, nor the taxes increased, so that the new may, in the least possible time, be thoroughly incorporated with the ancient state.

But when states are acquired in a country differing in language, customs, and laws, then come the difficulties, and then it requires great good fortune and much sagacity to hold them; and one of the best and most efficient means is for the prince who has acquired them to go and reside there, which will make his possession more secure and durable. Such was the course adopted by the Turk in Greece, who even if he had respected all the institutions of that country, yet could not possibly have succeeded in holding it, if he had not gone to reside there. For being on the spot, you can quickly remedy disorders as you see them arise; but not being there, you do not hear of them until they have become so great that there is no longer any remedy for them. Besides this, the country will not be despoiled by your officials, and the subjects will be satisfied by the easy recourse to the prince who is near them, which contributes to win their affections, if they are well disposed, and to inspire them with fear, if otherwise. And other powers will hesitate to assail a state where the prince himself resides, as they would find it very difficult to dispossess him.

The next best means for holding a newly acquired state is to establish colonies in one or two places that are as it were the keys to the country. Unless this is done, it will be necessary to keep a large force of men-at-arms and infantry there for its protection. Colonies are not very expensive to the prince; they can be established and maintained at little, if any, cost to him; and only those of the inhabitants will be injured by him whom he deprives of their homes and fields, for the purpose of bestowing them upon the colonists; and this will be the case only with a very small minority of the original inhabitants. And as those who are thus injured by him become dispersed and poor, they can never do him any harm, while all the other inhabitants remain on the one hand uninjured, and therefore easily kept quiet, and on the other hand they are afraid to stir, lest they should be despoiled as the others have been. I conclude then that such colonies are inexpensive, and are more faithful to the prince and less injurious to the inhabitants generally; while those who are injured by their establishment become poor and dispersed, and therefore unable to do any harm, as I have already said. And here we must observe that men must either be cajoled or crushed; for they will revenge themselves for slight wrongs, while for grave ones they cannot. The injury therefore that you do to a man should be such that you need not fear his revenge.

But if instead of colonies an armed force be sent for the preservation of a newly acquired province, then it will involve much greater expenditures, so that the support of such a guard may consume the entire revenue of the province; so that this acquisition may prove an actual loss, and will moreover give greater offense, because the whole population will feel aggrieved by having the armed force quartered upon them in turn. Every one that is made to suffer from this inconvenience will become an enemy; and these are enemies that can injure the prince, for although beaten yet they remain in their homes. In every point of view, then, such a military guard is disadvantageous, just as colonies are most useful.

A prince, moreover, who wishes to keep possession of a country that is separate and unlike his own, must make himself the chief and protector of the smaller neighboring powers. He must endeavor to weaken the most powerful of them, and must take care that by no chance a stranger[1] enter that province who is equally powerful with himself; for strangers are never called in except by those whom an undue ambition or fear have rendered malcontents. It was thus in fact that the Ætolians called the Romans into Greece; and whatever other country the Romans entered, it was invariably at the request of the inhabitants.

The way in which these things happen is generally thus:

---

[1] i.e., a foreign power.

so soon as a powerful foreigner enters a province, all those of its inhabitants that are less powerful will give him their adhesion, being influenced thereto by their jealousy of him who has hitherto been their superior. So that, as regards these petty lords, the new prince need not be at any trouble to win them over to himself, as they will all most readily become incorporated with the state which he has there acquired. He has merely to see to it that they do not assume too much authority, or acquire too much power; for he will then be able by their favor, and by his own strength, very easily to humble those who are really powerful; so that he will in all respects remain the sole arbiter of that province. And he who does not manage this part well will quickly lose what he has acquired; and while he holds it, he will experience infinite difficulties and vexations. The Romans observed these points most carefully in the provinces which they conquered; they established colonies there, and sustained the feebler chiefs without increasing their power, while they humbled the stronger, and permitted no powerful stranger to acquire any influence or credit there. I will confine myself for an example merely to the provinces of Greece. The Romans sustained the Achaians and the Ætolians, while they humbled the kingdom of Macedon and expelled Antiochus from his dominions; but neither the merits of the Achaians or of the Ætolians caused the Romans to permit either of them to increase in power; nor could the persuasions of Philip induce the Romans to become his friends until after first having humbled his power; nor could the power of Antiochus make them consent that he should hold any state in that province.

Thus in all these cases the Romans did what all wise princes ought to do; namely, not only to look to all present troubles, but also to those of the future, against which they provided with the utmost prudence. For it is by foreseeing difficulties from afar that they are easily provided against; but awaiting their near approach, remedies are no longer in time, for the malady has become incurable. It happens in such cases, as the doctors say of consumption, that in the early stages it is easy to cure, but difficult to recognize; while in the course of time, the disease not having been recognized and cured in the beginning, it becomes easy to know, but difficult to cure. And thus it is in the affairs of state; for when the evils that arise in it are seen far ahead, which it is given only to a wise prince to do, then they are easily remedied; but when, in consequence of not having been foreseen, these evils are allowed to grow and assume such proportions that they become manifest to every one, then they can no longer be remedied.

The Romans therefore, on seeing troubles far ahead, always strove to avert them in time, and never permitted their growth merely for the sake of avoiding a war, well knowing that the war would not be prevented, and that to defer it would only be an advantage to others; and for these reasons they resolved upon attacking Philip and Antiochus in Greece, so as to prevent these from making war upon them in Italy. They might at the time have avoided both the one and the other, but would not do it; nor did they ever fancy the saying which is nowadays in the mouth of every wiseacre, "to bide the advantages of time," but preferred those of their own valor and prudence;

for time drives all things before it, and may lead to good as well as to evil, and to evil as well as to good.

But let us return to France, and examine whether she has done any one of the things that we have spoken of. I will say nothing of Charles VIII, but only of Louis XII, whose proceedings we are better able to understand, as he held possession of Italy for a greater length of time. And we shall see how he did the very opposite of what he should have done, for the purpose of holding a state so unlike his own.

King Louis XII was called into Italy by the ambition of the Venetians, who wanted him to aid them in conquering a portion of Lombardy. I will not blame the King for the part he took; for, wishing to gain a foothold in Italy, and having no allies there, but rather finding the gates everywhere closed against him in consequence of the conduct of King Charles VIII, he was obliged to avail himself of such friends as he could find; and would have succeeded in his attempt, which was well planned, but for an error which he committed in his subsequent conduct. The King, then, having conquered Lombardy, quickly recovered that prestige which his predecessor, Charles VIII, had lost. Genoa yielded; the Florentines became his friends; the Marquis of Mantua, the Duke of Ferrara, the Bentivogli, the lady of Furli, the lords of Faenza, Pesaro, Rimini, Camerino, and Piombino, the Lucchese, the Pisanese, and the Sienese, all came to meet him with offers of friendship. The Venetians might then have recognized the folly of their course, when, for the sake of gaining two cities in Lombardy, they made King Louis master of two thirds of Italy.

Let us see now how easily the King might have maintained his influence in Italy if he had observed the rules above given. Had he secured and protected all these friends of his, who were numerous but feeble,—some fearing the Church, and some the Venetians, and therefore all forced to adhere to him,—he might easily have secured himself against the remaining stronger powers of Italy. But no sooner was he in Milan than he did the very opposite, by giving aid to Pope Alexander VI to enable him to seize the Romagna. Nor did he perceive that in doing this he weakened himself, by alienating his friends and those who had thrown themselves into his arms; and that he had made the Church great by adding so much temporal to its spiritual power, which gave it already so much authority. Having committed this first error, he was obliged to follow it up; so that, for the purpose of putting an end to the ambition of Pope Alexander VI, and preventing his becoming master of Tuscany, he was obliged to come into Italy.

Not content with having made the Church great, and with having alienated his own friends, King Louis, in his eagerness to possess the kingdom of Naples, shared it with the King of Spain; so that where he had been the sole arbiter of Italy, he established an associate and rival, to whom the ambitious and the malcontents might have a ready recourse. And while he could have left a king in Naples who would have been his tributary, he dispossessed him, for the sake of replacing him by another who was powerful enough in turn to drive him out.

The desire of conquest is certainly most natural and common among men, and whenever they yield to it and are successful, they are praised, or at least not blamed; but when they lack the means, and yet attempt it anyhow, then they commit an error that merits blame. If, then, the King of France was powerful enough by himself successfully to attack the kingdom of Naples, then he was right to do so; but if he was not, then he should not have divided it with the King of Spain. And if the partition of Lombardy with the Venetians was excusable because it enabled him to gain a foothold in Italy, that of Naples with the Spaniard deserves censure, as it cannot be excused on the ground of necessity.

Louis XII then committed these five errors: he destroyed the weak; he increased the power of one already powerful in Italy; he established a most powerful stranger there; he did not go to reside there himself; nor did he plant any colonies there. These errors, however, would not have injured him during his lifetime, had he not committed a sixth one in attempting to deprive the Venetians of their possessions. For if Louis had not increased the power of the Church, nor established the Spaniards in Italy, it would have been quite reasonable, and even advisable, for him to have weakened the Venetians; but having done both those things, he ought never to have consented to their ruin; for so long as the Venetians were powerful, they would always have kept others from any attempt upon Lombardy. They would on the one hand never have permitted this unless it should have led to their becoming masters of it, and on the other hand no one would have taken it from France for the sake of giving it to the Venetians; nor would any one have had the courage to attack the French and the Venetians combined. And should it be said that King Louis gave up the Romagna to Pope

Alexander VI, and divided the kingdom of Naples with the Spaniard for the sake of avoiding a war, then I reply with the above stated reasons, that no one should ever submit to an evil for the sake of avoiding a war. For a war is never avoided, but is only deferred to one's own disadvantage.

And should it be argued, on the other hand, that the King felt bound by the pledge which he had given to the Pope to conquer the Romagna for him in consideration of his dissolving the King's marriage, and of his bestowing the cardinal's hat upon the Archbishop of Rouen, then I meet that argument with what I shall say further on concerning the pledges of princes, and the manner in which they should keep them.

King Louis then lost Lombardy by not having conformed to any one of the conditions that have been observed by others, who, having conquered provinces, wanted to keep them. Nor is this at all to be wondered at, for it is quite reasonable and common. I conversed on this subject with the Archbishop of Rouen (Cardinal d'Amboise) while at Nantes, when the Duke Valentino, commonly called Cesare Borgia, son of Pope Alexander VI, made himself master of the Romagna. On that occasion the Cardinal said to me, that the Italians did not understand the art of war. To which I replied that the French did not understand statesmanship; for if they had understood it, they would never have allowed the Church to attain such greatness and power. For experience proves that the greatness of the Church and that of Spain in Italy were brought about by France, and that her own ruin resulted therefrom. From this we draw the general rule, which never or rarely fails, that the prince who causes another to become powerful thereby works his own ruin; for he has contributed to the power of the other either by his own ability or force, and both the one and the other will be mistrusted by him whom he has thus made powerful.

CHAPTER IV

WHY THE KINGDOM OF DARIUS, WHICH WAS CONQUERED BY ALEXANDER, DID NOT REVOLT AGAINST THE SUCCESSORS OF ALEXANDER AFTER HIS DEATH

If we reflect upon the difficulties of preserving a newly acquired state, it seems marvellous that, after the rapid conquest of all Asia by Alexander the Great, and his subsequent death, which one would suppose most naturally to have provoked the whole country to revolt, his successors nonetheless maintained their possession of it, and experienced no other difficulties in holding it than such as arose among themselves from their own ambition.

I meet this observation by saying that all principalities of which we have any accounts have been governed in one of two ways; viz. either by one absolute prince, to whom all others are as slaves, some of whom, as ministers, by his grace and consent, aid him in the government of his realm; or else by a prince and nobles, who hold that rank, not by the grace of their sovereign, but by the antiquity of their lineage. Such nobles have estates and subjects of their own, who recognize them as their liege lords, and have a natural affection for them.

In those states that are governed by an absolute prince and slaves, the prince has far more power and authority; for in his entire dominion no one recognizes any other superior but him; and if they obey any one else, they do it as though to his minister and officer, and without any particular affection for such official. Turkey and France furnish us examples of these two different systems of government at the present time. The whole country of the Turk is governed by one master; all the rest are his slaves; and having divided the country into Sanjacs, or districts, he appoints governors for each of these, whom he changes and replaces at his pleasure.

But the King of France is placed in the midst of a large number of ancient nobles, who are recognized and acknowledged by their subjects as their lords, and are held in great affection by them. They have their rank and prerogatives, of which the King cannot deprive them without danger to himself. In observing now these two principalities, we perceive the difficulty of conquering the empire of the Turk, but once conquered it will be very easily held. The reasons that make the conquest of the Turkish empire so difficult are, that the conqueror cannot be called into the country by any of the great nobles of the state; nor can he hope that his attempt could be facilitated by a revolt of those who surround the sovereign; which arises from the above given reasons. For being all slaves and dependants of their sovereign, it is more difficult to corrupt them; and even if they were corrupted, but little advantage could be hoped for from them, because they cannot carry the people along with them.

Whoever therefore attacks the Turks must expect to find them united, and must depend wholly upon his own forces, and not upon any internal disturbances. But once having defeated and driven the Turk from the field, so that he cannot reorganize his army, then he will have nothing to fear but the line of the sovereign. This however once extinguished, the conqueror has nothing to apprehend from any one else, as none other has any influence with the people; and thus, having had nothing to hope from them before the victory, he will have nothing to fear from them afterward.

The contrary takes place in kingdoms governed like that of France; for having gained over some of the great nobles of the realm, there will be no difficulty in entering it, there being always malcontents and others who desire a change. These, for the reasons stated, can open the way into the country for the assailant, and facilitate his success. But for the conqueror to maintain himself there afterward will involve infinite difficulties, both with the conquered and with those who have aided him in his conquest. Nor will it suffice to extinguish the line of the sovereign, because the great nobles remain, who will place themselves at the head of new movements; and the conqueror, not being able either to satisfy or to crush them, will lose the country again on the first occasion that presents itself.

If now we consider the nature of the government of Darius, we shall find that it resembled that of the Turk, and therefore it was necessary for Alexander to attack him in full force, and drive him from the field. After this victory and the death of Darius, Alexander remained in secure possession of the kingdom for the reasons above explained. And if his successors had remained united, they

16

might also have enjoyed possession at their ease; for no other disturbances occurred in that empire, except such as they created themselves.

Countries, however, with a system of government like that of France, cannot possibly be held so easily. The frequent insurrections of Spain, France, and Greece against the Romans were due to the many petty princes that existed in those states; and therefore, so long as the memory of these princes endured, the Romans were ever uncertain in the tenure of those states. But all remembrance of these princes once effaced, the Romans became secure possessors of those countries, so long as the growth and power of their empire endured. And even afterward, when fighting among themselves, each of the parties were able to keep for themselves portions of those countries, according to the authority which they had acquired there; and the line of their sovereigns being extinguished, the inhabitants recognized no other authority but that of the Romans.

Reflecting now upon these things, we cannot be surprised at the facility with which Alexander maintained himself in Asia; nor at the difficulties which others experienced in preserving their conquests, as was the case with Pyrrhus and many others, and which resulted not from the greater or lesser valor of the conqueror, but from the different nature of the conquered states.

CHAPTER V

Conquered states that have been accustomed to liberty and
the government of their own laws can be held by the conqueror in three different ways. The first is to ruin them;
the second, for the conqueror to go and reside there in
person; and the third is to allow them to continue to live
under their own laws, subject to a regular tribute, and to
create in them a government of a few, who will keep the
country friendly to the conqueror. Such a government,
having been established by the new prince, knows that it
cannot maintain itself without the support of his power
and friendship, and it becomes its interest therefore to
sustain him. A city that has been accustomed to free
institutions is much easier held by its own citizens than in
any other way, if the conqueror desires to preserve it. The
Spartans and the Romans will serve as examples of these
different ways of holding a conquered state.

The Spartans held Athens and Thebes, creating there
a government of a few; and yet they lost both these states
again. The Romans, for the purpose of retaining Capua,
Carthage, and Numantia, destroyed them, but did not
lose them. They wished to preserve Greece in somewhat

the same way that the Spartans had held it, by making her free and leaving her in the enjoyment of her own laws, but did not succeed; so that they were obliged to destroy many cities in that country for the purpose of holding it. In truth there was no other safe way of keeping possession of that country but to ruin it. And whoever becomes master of a city that has been accustomed to liberty, and does not destroy it, must himself expect to be ruined by it. For they will always resort to rebellion in the name of liberty and their ancient institutions, which will never be effaced from their memory, either by the lapse of time, or by benefits bestowed by the new master. No matter what he may do, or what precautions he may take, if he does not separate and disperse the inhabitants, they will on the first occasion invoke the name of liberty and the memory of their ancient institutions, as was done by Pisa after having been held over a hundred years in subjection by the Florentines.

But it is very different with states that have been accustomed to live under a prince. When the line of the prince is once extinguished, the inhabitants, being on the one hand accustomed to obey, and on the other having lost their ancient sovereign, can neither agree to create a new one from among themselves, nor do they know how to live in liberty; and thus they will be less prompt to take up arms, and the new prince will readily be able to gain their good will and to assure himself of them. But republics have more vitality, a greater spirit of resentment and desire of revenge, for the memory of their ancient liberty neither can nor will permit them to remain quiet, and therefore the surest way of holding them is either to destroy them, or for the conqueror to go and live there.

CHAPTER VI

*OF NEW PRINCIPALITIES THAT HAVE
BEEN ACQUIRED BY THE VALOR OF THE
PRINCE AND BY HIS OWN TROOPS*

Let no one wonder if, in what I am about to say of entirely new principalities and of the prince and his government, I cite the very highest examples. For as men almost always follow the beaten track of others, and proceed in their actions by imitation, and yet cannot altogether follow the ways of others, nor attain the high qualities of those whom they imitate, so a wise man should ever follow the ways of great men and endeavor to imitate only such as have been most eminent; so that even if his merits do not quite equal theirs, yet that they may in some measure reflect their greatness. He should do as the skillful archer, who, seeing that the object he desires to hit is too distant, and knowing the extent to which his bow will carry, aims higher than the destined mark, not for the purpose of sending his arrow to that height, but so that by this elevation it may reach the desired aim.

I say then that a new prince in an entirely new principality will experience more or less difficulty in maintaining himself, according as he has more or less courage and ability. And as such an event as to become a prince from a mere private individual presupposes either great courage or rare good fortune, it would seem that one or the other of these two causes ought in a measure to mitigate many of these difficulties. But he who depends least upon fortune will maintain himself best; which will be still more easy for the Prince if, having no other state, he is obliged to reside in his newly acquired principality.

To come now to those who by their courage and ability, and not by fortune, have risen to the rank of rulers, I will say that the most eminent of such were Moses, Cyrus, Romulus, Theseus, and the like. And although we may not discuss Moses, who was a mere executor of the things ordained by God, yet he merits our admiration, if only for that grace which made him worthy to hold direct communion with the Almighty. But if we consider Cyrus and others who have conquered or founded empires, we shall find them all worthy of admiration; for if we study their acts and particular ordinances, they do not seem very different from those of Moses, although he had so great a teacher. We shall also find in examining their acts and lives, that they had no other favor from fortune but opportunity, which gave them the material which they could mold into whatever form seemed to them best; and without such opportunity the great qualities of their souls would have been wasted, while without those great qualities the opportunities would have been in vain.

It was necessary then for Moses to find the people of Israel slaves in Egypt, and oppressed by the Egyptians, so that to escape from that bondage they resolved to follow him. It was necessary that Romulus should not have been kept in Alba, and that he should have been exposed at his birth, for him to have become the founder and King of Rome. And so it was necessary for Cyrus to find the Persians dissatisfied with the rule of the Medes, and the Medes effeminate and enfeebled by long peace. And finally, Theseus could not have manifested his courage had he not found the Athenians dispersed. These opportunities therefore made these men fortunate, and it was their lofty personal courage and talents that enabled them to recognize the opportunities by which their countries were made illustrious and most happy. Those who by similar noble conduct become princes acquire their principalities with difficulty, but maintain them with ease; and the difficulties which they experience in acquiring their principalities arise in part from the new ordinances and customs which they are obliged to introduce for the purpose of founding their state and their own security. We must bear in mind, then, that there is nothing more difficult and dangerous, or more doubtful of success, than an attempt to introduce a new order of things in any state. For the innovator has for enemies all those who derived advantages from the old order of things while those who expect to be benefited by the new institutions will be but lukewarm defenders. This indifference arises in part from fear of their adversaries who were favored by the existing laws, and partly from the incredulity of men who have no faith in anything new that is not the result of well-established experience. Hence it is that, whenever the opponents of the new order of things have the opportunity to attack it, they will do it with the zeal of partisans, while the others defend it but feebly, so that it is dangerous to rely upon the latter.

If we desire to discuss this subject thoroughly, it will be necessary to examine whether such innovators depend upon themselves, or whether they rely upon others; that is to say, whether for the purpose of carrying out their plans they have to resort to entreaties, or whether they can accomplish it by force. In the first case they always succeed badly, and fail to conclude anything; but when they depend upon their own strength to carry their innovations through, then they rarely incur any danger. Thence it was that all prophets who came with arms in hand were successful, while those who were not armed were ruined. For besides the reasons given above, the dispositions of peoples are variable; it is easy to persuade them to anything, but difficult to confirm them in that belief. And therefore a prophet should be prepared, in case the people will not believe any more, to be able by force to compel them to that belief.

Neither Moses, Cyrus, Theseus, nor Romulus would have been able to make their laws and institutions observed for any length of time, if they had not been prepared to enforce them with arms. This was the experience of Brother Girolamo Savonarola, who failed in his attempt to establish a new order of things so soon as the multitude ceased to believe in him; for he had not the means to keep his believers firm in their faith, nor to make the unbelievers believe. And yet these great men experienced great difficulties in their course, and met danger at every step, which could only be overcome by their courage and ability. But once having surmounted them, then they began to be held in veneration; and having crushed those who were jealous of their great qualities, they remained powerful, secure, honored, and happy.

To these great examples I will add a minor one, which nevertheless bears some relation to them, and will suffice me for all similar cases. This is Hiero of Syracuse, who from a mere private individual rose to be prince of Syracuse, although he owed no other favor to fortune than opportunity; for the Syracusans, being oppressed, elected him their captain, whence he advanced by his merits to become their prince. And even in his condition as a private citizen he displayed such virtue, that the author who wrote of him said that he lacked nothing of being a monarch excepting a kingdom. Hiero disbanded the old army and organized a new one; he abandoned his old allies and formed new alliances; and having thus an army and allies of his own creation, he had no difficulty in erecting any edifice upon such a foundation; so that although he had much trouble in attaining the principality, yet he had but little in maintaining it.

CHAPTER VII

OF NEW PRINCIPALITIES THAT HAVE BEEN ACQUIRED BY THE AID OF OTHERS AND BY GOOD FORTUNE

Those who by good fortune only rise from mere private station to the dignity of princes have but little trouble in achieving that elevation, for they fly there as it were on wings; but their difficulties begin after they have been placed in that high position. Such are those who acquire a state either by means of money, or by the favor of some powerful monarch who bestows it upon them. Many such instances occurred in Greece, in the cities of Ionia and

of the Hellespont, where men were made princes by
Darius so that they might hold those places for his security
and glory. And such were those Emperors who from
having been mere private individuals attained the Empire
by corrupting the soldiery. These remain simply subject
to the will and the fortune of those who bestowed greatness upon them, which are two most uncertain and variable
things. And generally these men have neither the skill
nor the power to maintain that high rank. They know not
(for unless they are men of great genius and ability, it is
not reasonable that they should know) how to command,
having never occupied any but private stations; and they
cannot, because they have no troops upon whose loyalty
and attachment they can depend.

Moreover, states that spring up suddenly, like other
things in nature that are born and attain their growth
rapidly, cannot have those roots and supports that will
protect them from destruction by the first unfavorable
weather. Unless indeed, as has been said, those who have
suddenly become princes are gifted with such ability that
they quickly know how to prepare themselves for the
preservation of that which fortune has cast into their lap,
and afterward to build up those foundations which others
have laid before becoming princes.

In illustration of the one and the other of these two
ways of becoming princes, by valor and ability, or by
good fortune, I will adduce two examples from the time
within our own memory; these are Francesco Sforza and
Cesare Borgia. Francesco, by legitimate means and by
great natural ability, rose from a private citizen to be
Duke of Milan; and having attained that high position by

a thousand efforts, it cost him but little trouble afterward to maintain it. On the other hand, Cesare Borgia, commonly called Duke Valentino, acquired his state by the good fortune of his father, but lost it when no longer sustained by that good fortune; although he employed all the means and did all that a brave and prudent man can do to take root in that state which had been bestowed upon him by the arms and good fortune of another. For, as we have said above, he who does not lay the foundations for his power beforehand may be able by great ability and courage to do so afterward; but it will be done with great trouble to the builder and with danger to the edifice.

If now we consider the whole course of the Duke Valentino, we shall see that he took pains to lay solid foundations for his future power; which I think it well to discuss. For I should not know what better lesson I could give to a new prince, than to hold up to him the example of the Duke Valentino's conduct. And if the measures which he adopted did not insure his final success, the fault was not his, for his failure was due to the extreme and extraordinary malignity of fortune. Pope Alexander VI in his efforts to aggrandize his son, the Duke Valentino, encountered many difficulties, immediate and prospective. In the first place he saw that there was no chance of making him master of any state, unless a state of the Church; and he knew that neither the Duke of Milan nor the Venetians would consent to that. Faenza and Rimini were already at that time under the protection of the Venetians; and the armies of Italy, especially those of which he could have availed himself, were in the hands of men who had cause to fear the power of the Pope, namely the Orsini, the Colonna, and their adherents; and therefore he could not rely upon them.

It became necessary therefore for Alexander to disturb the existing order of things, and to disorganize those states, in order to make himself safely master of them. And this it was easy for him to do; for he found the Venetians, influenced by other reasons, favorable to the return of the French into Italy; which not only he did not oppose, but facilitated by dissolving the former marriage of King Louis XII (so as to enable him to marry Ann of Brittany). The King thereupon entered Italy with the aid of the Venetians and the consent of Alexander; and no sooner was he in Milan than the Pope obtained troops from him to aid in the conquest of the Romagna, which was yielded to him through the influence of the King.

The Duke Valentino having thus acquired the Romagna, and the Colonna being discouraged, he both wished to hold that province, and also to push his possessions still further, but was prevented by two circumstances. The one was that his own troops seemed to him not to be reliable, and the other was the will of the King of France. That is to say, he feared lest the Orsini troops, which he had made use of, might fail him at the critical moment, and not only prevent him from acquiring more, but even take from him that which he had acquired; and that even the King of France might do the same. Of the disposition of the Orsini, the Duke had a proof when, after the capture of Faenza, he attacked Bologna, and saw with what indifference they moved to the assault. And as to the King of France, he knew his mind; for when he wanted to march into Tuscany, after having taken the Duchy of Urbino, King Louis made him desist from that undertaking. The Duke resolved therefore to rely no longer upon the fortune or the arms of others. And the first thing he did was to weaken the Orsini and the Colonna in Rome, by winning over to himself all the gentlemen adherents of those houses, by taking them into his own pay as gentlemen followers, giving them liberal stipends and bestowing honors upon them in proportion to their condition, and giving them appointments and commands; so that in the course of a few months their attachment to their factions was extinguished, and they all became devoted followers of the Duke.

After that, having successfully dispersed the Colonna faction, he watched for an opportunity to crush the Orsini, which soon presented itself, and of which he made the most. For the Orsini, having been slow to perceive that the aggrandizement of the Duke and of the Church would prove the cause of their ruin, convened a meeting at Magione, in the Perugine territory, which gave rise to the revolt of Urbino and the disturbances in the Romagna, and caused infinite dangers to the Duke Valentino, all of which, however, he overcame with the aid of the French. Having thus re-established his reputation, and trusting no longer in the French or any other foreign power, he had recourse to deceit, so as to avoid putting them to the test. And so well did he know how to dissemble and conceal his intentions that the Orsini became reconciled to him, through the agency of Signor Paolo, whom the Duke had won over to himself by means of all possible good offices, and gifts of money, clothing, and horses. And thus their credulity led them into the hands of the Duke at Sinigaglia.[1]

The chiefs thus destroyed, and their adherents converted into his friends, the Duke had laid sufficiently good foundations for his power, having made himself master of the whole of the Romagna and the Duchy of Urbino, and having attached their entire population to himself, by giving them a foretaste of the new prosperity which they were to enjoy under him. And as this part of the Duke's proceedings is well worthy of notice, and may serve as an example to others, I will dwell upon it more fully.

Having conquered the Romagna, the Duke found it under the control of a number of impotent petty tyrants, who had devoted themselves more to plundering their subjects than to governing them properly, and encouraging discord and disorder among them rather than peace and union; so that this province was infested by brigands, torn by quarrels, and given over to every sort of violence. He saw at once that, to restore order among the inhabitants and obedience to the sovereign, it was necessary to establish a good and vigorous government there. And for this purpose he appointed as governor of that province Don Ramiro d' Orco, a man of cruelty, but at the same time of great energy, to whom he gave plenary power. In a very short time D' Orco reduced the province to peace and order, thereby gaining for him the highest reputation. After a while the Duke found such excessive exercise of authority no longer necessary or expedient, for he feared that it might render himself odious. He therefore established a civil tribunal in the heart of the province, under

---

[1] Where they were strangled in cold blood.

an excellent president, where every city should have its own advocate. And having observed that the past rigor of Ramiro had engendered some hatred, he wished to show to the people, for the purpose of removing that feeling from their minds, and to win their entire confidence, that, if any cruelties had been practiced, they had not originated with him, but had resulted altogether from the harsh nature of his minister. He therefore took occasion to have Messer Ramiro put to death, and his body, cut into two parts, exposed in the market-place of Cesena one morning, with a block of wood and a bloody cutlass left beside him. The horror of this spectacle caused the people to remain for a time stupefied and satisfied.

But let us return to where we started from. I say, then, that the Duke, feeling himself strong enough now, and in a measure secure from immediate danger, having raised an armed force of his own, and having in great part destroyed those that were near and might have troubled him, wanted now to proceed with his conquest. The only power remaining which he had to fear was the King of France, upon whose support he knew that he could not count, although the King had been late in discovering his error of having allowed the Duke's aggrandizement. The Duke, therefore, began to look for new alliances, and to prevaricate with the French about their entering the kingdom of Naples for the purpose of attacking the Spaniards, who were then engaged in the siege of Gaeta. His intention was to place them in such a position that they would not be able to harm him; and in this he would have succeeded easily if Pope Alexander had lived.

Such was the course of the Duke Valentino with regard to the immediate present, but he had cause for apprehensions as to the future; mainly, lest the new successor to the papal chair should not be friendly to him, and should attempt to take from him what had been given him by Alexander. And this he thought of preventing in several different ways: one, by extirpating the families of those whom he had despoiled, so as to deprive the Pope of all pretext of restoring them to their possessions; secondly, by gaining over to himself all the nobility of Rome, so as to be able, through them, to keep the Pope in check; thirdly, by getting the College of Cardinals under his control; and, fourthly, by acquiring so much power before the death of Alexander that he might by himself be able to resist the first attack of his enemies. Of these four things he had accomplished three at the time of Alexander's death; for of the petty tyrants whom he had despoiled he had killed as many as he could lay hands on, and but very few had been able to save themselves; he had won over to himself the nobility of Rome, and had secured a large majority in the sacred college; and as to further acquisitions, he contemplated making himself master of Tuscany, having already possession of Perugia and Piombino, and having assumed a protectorate over Pisa. There being no longer occasion to be apprehensive of France, which had been deprived of the kingdom of Naples by the Spaniards, so that both of these powers had to seek his friendship, he suddenly seized Pisa. After this, Lucca and Siena promptly yielded to him, partly from jealousy of the Florentines and partly from fear. Thus Florence saw no safety from the Duke, and if he had succeeded in taking that city, as he could have done in the very year of Alexander's death, it would have so increased his power and influence that he would have been able to have sustained himself alone, without depending upon the fortune or power of any one else, and relying solely upon his own strength and courage.

But Alexander died five years after the Duke had first unsheathed his sword. He left his son with only his government of the Romagna firmly established, but all his other possessions entirely uncertain, hemmed in between two powerful hostile armies, and himself sick unto death. But such were the Duke's energy and courage, and so well did he know how men are either won or destroyed, and so solid were the foundations which he had in so brief a time laid for his greatness, that if he had not had these two armies upon his back, and had been in health, he would have sustained himself against all difficulties. And that the foundations of his power were well laid may be judged by the fact that the Romagna remained faithful, and waited quietly for him more than a month; and that, although half dead with sickness, yet he was perfectly secure in Rome; and that, although the Baglioni, Vitelli, and Orsini came to Rome at the time, yet they could not raise a party against him. Unable to make a Pope of his own choice, yet he could prevent the election of any one that was not acceptable to him. And had the Duke been in health at the time of Alexander's death, everything would have gone well with him; for he said to me on the day when Julius II was created Pope, that he had provided for everything that could possibly occur in case of his father's death, except that he never thought that at that moment he should himself be so near dying.

Upon reviewing now all the actions of the Duke, I should not know where to blame him; it seems to me that I should rather hold him up as an example (as I have said) to be imitated by all those who have risen to sovereignty, either by the good fortune or the arms of others. For being endowed with great courage, and having a lofty ambition, he could not have acted otherwise under the circumstances; and the only thing that defeated his designs was the shortness of Alexander's life and his own bodily infirmity.

Whoever, then, in a newly acquired state, finds it necessary to secure himself against his enemies, to gain friends, to conquer by force or by cunning, to make himself feared or beloved by the people, to be followed and revered by the soldiery, to destroy all who could or might injure him, to substitute a new for the old order of things, to be severe and yet gracious, magnanimous, and liberal, to disband a disloyal army and create a new one, to preserve the friendship of kings and princes, so that they may bestow benefits upon him with grace, and fear to injure him,—such a one, I say, cannot find more recent examples than those presented by the conduct of the Duke Valentino. The only thing we can blame him for was the election of Julius II to the pontificate, which was a bad selection for him to make; for, as has been said, though he was not able to make a Pope to his own liking, yet he could have prevented, and should never have consented to, the election of one from among those cardinals whom he had offended, or who, if he had been elected, would have had occasion to fear him, for either fear or resentment makes men enemies.

Those whom the Duke had offended were, among others, the Cardinals San Pietro in Vincola, Colonna, San Giorgio, and Ascanio. All the others, had they come to the pontificate, would have had to fear him, excepting

D'Amboise and the Spanish cardinals; the latter because of certain relations and reciprocal obligations, and the former because of his power, he having France for his ally. The Duke then should by all means have had one of the Spanish cardinals made Pope, and failing in that, he should have supported the election of the Cardinal d'Amboise, and not that of the Cardinal San Pietro in Vincola. For whoever thinks that among great personages recent benefits will cause old injuries to be forgotten, deceives himself greatly. The Duke, then, in consenting to the election of Julius II, committed an error which proved the cause of his ultimate ruin.

CHAPTER VIII

OF SUCH AS HAVE ACHIEVED
SOVEREIGNTY BY MEANS OF CRIMES

But as there are also two ways in which a person may rise from private station to sovereignty, and which can neither be attributed to fortune nor to valor, it seems to me they should not be left unnoticed; although one of these ways might be more fully discussed when we treat of republics. These two modes are, when one achieves sovereignty either by wicked and nefarious means, or when a private citizen becomes sovereign of his country by the favor of his fellow-citizens. I will explain the first by two examples, the one ancient and the other modern;

The Prince

and without entering otherwise into the merits of these cases, I judge they will suffice to any one who may find himself obliged to imitate them.

Agathocles, a Sicilian, rose to be King of Syracuse, not only from being a mere private citizen, but from the lowest and most abject condition. He was the son of a potter, and led a vicious life through all the various phases of his career. But his wickedness was coupled with so much moral and physical courage, that, having joined the army, he rose by successive steps until he became Prætor of Syracuse. Having attained that rank he resolved to make himself sovereign, and to retain by violence, and regardless of others, that which had been intrusted to him by public consent. For this purpose he came to an understanding with Hamilcar the Carthaginian, who was at that time carrying on war with his army in Sicily; and having one morning called an assembly of the people and the Senate of Syracuse, as though he wished to confer with them about public affairs, he made his soldiers, at a given signal, slay all the senators and the richest of the people, and then seized the sovereignty of that city without any resistance on the part of the citizens. Although afterward twice defeated by the Carthaginians, and finally besieged by them in Syracuse, he not only defended that city, but, leaving a portion of his forces to sustain the siege, he crossed the sea with the other part and attacked Africa, thus raising the siege of Syracuse in a short time, and driving the Carthaginians to the extremest necessity, compelling them to make terms with him, and to remain content with the possession of Africa, and leave Sicily to him.

Whoever now reflects upon the conduct and valor of

35

Agathocles will find in them little or nothing that can be attributed to fortune; for, as I have said, he achieved sovereignty, not by the favor of any one, but through his high rank in the army, which he had won by a thousand efforts and dangers, and he afterward maintained his sovereignty with great courage, and even temerity. And yet we cannot call it valor to massacre one's fellow-citizens, to betray one's friends, and to be devoid of good faith, mercy, and religion; such means may enable a man to achieve empire, but not glory. Still, if we consider the valor of Agathocles in encountering and overcoming dangers, and his invincible courage in supporting and mastering adversity, we shall find no reason why he should be regarded inferior to any of the most celebrated captains. But with all this, his outrageous cruelty and in- humanity, together with his infinite crimes, will not permit him to be classed with the most celebrated men. We can- not therefore ascribe to either valor or fortune the achieve- ments of Agathocles, which he accomplished without either the one or the other.

In our own times, during the pontificate of Alexander VI, Oliverotto da Fermo, having been left an orphan, was brought up by his maternal uncle, Giovanni Fogliani, and was in early youth placed in the military service under Paolo Vitelli; so that, after having been thoroughly trained and disciplined, he might attain prominent rank in the army. After the death of Paolo, he served under his brother Vitellozzo; and became in a very short time, by his intelligence, his bodily strength and intrepidity, one of the foremost men in the service. But deeming it servile to act under the command of others, he planned, to- gether with some of the citizens of Fermo who preferred servitude to the liberty of their country, and with the concurrence of Vitellozzo, to seize Fermo and make himself lord of the same. With this object he wrote to his uncle, Giovanni Fogliani, that, having been absent from home for several years, he desired now to come to see him and his native city, and also to look up his patrimony; and that, having until then striven only to acquire honor, he desired to show his fellow-citizens that he had not labored in vain; and therefore he wished to come in splendid style, accompanied by one hundred cavaliers, friends of his. He begged his uncle, therefore, to be pleased to arrange that the inhabitants of Fermo should give him an honorable reception, which would be an honor not only to him but also to Giovanni, who was his near relative and had brought him up. Giovanni therefore omitted no courtesies due to his nephew, and caused the citizens of Fermo to give him an honorable reception, as well as lodgings in their houses for himself and all his retinue. After spending some days in Fermo, and arranging all that was necessary for the execution of his villainous design, Oliverotto gave a sumptuous entertainment, to which he invited his uncle Giovanni and all the principal citizens of Fermo. After the dinner and the other entertainments that are customary on such occasions, Oliverotto artfully started a grave discussion respecting the greatness of Pope Alexander VI and his son Cesare Borgia and their enterprises. When Giovanni and the others replied to his remarks, Oliverotto suddenly arose, saying that these things were only to be spoken of in private places, and withdrew to another room, whither Giovanni and the other citizens followed. No sooner had they seated themselves there, than some of Oliverotto's soldiers rushed out from concealment and massacred Giovanni and all the others.

After this murder Oliverotto mounted his horse, rode through the streets of Fermo, and besieged the supreme magistrates in the palace, who, constrained by fear, obeyed him, and formed a government of which Oliverotto made himself sovereign. And as all those who, as malcontents, might have injured him, had been put to death, Oliverotto fortified himself in his position with new institutions, both civil and military, so that for the space of a year, during which he held the sovereignty, he was not only secure in the city of Fermo, but had become formidable to all his neighbors; so that it would have been as difficult to overcome him as Agathocles, had he not allowed himself to be deceived by Cesare Borgia, when, as I have related, he entrapped the Orsini and the Vitelli at Sinigaglia, where Oliverotto was also taken and strangled, together with Vitellozzo, his master in valor and in villainy, just one year after he had committed parricide in having his uncle Giovanni Fogliani assassinated.

Some may wonder how it was that Agathocles, and others like him, after their infinite treason and cruelty, could live for any length of time securely in the countries whose sovereignty they had usurped, and even defend themselves successfully against external enemies, without any attempts on the part of their own citizens to conspire against them; while many others could not by means of cruelty maintain their state even in time of peace, much less in doubtful times of war. I believe that this happened according as the cruelties were well or ill applied; we may call cruelty well applied (if indeed we may praise evil) when it is committed once from necessity for self-protection, and afterward not persisted in, but converted as far as possible to the public good. Ill-applied cruelties are those which, though at first but few, yet increase with time rather than cease altogether. Those who adopt the first practice may, with the help of God and man, render some service to their state, as had been done by Agathocles; but those who adopt the latter course will not possibly be able to maintain themselves in their state. Whence it is to be noted that in taking possession of a state the conqueror should well reflect as to the harsh measures that may be necessary, and then execute them at a single blow, so as not to be obliged to renew them every day; and by thus not repeating them, to assure himself of the support of the inhabitants, and win them over to himself by benefits bestowed. And he who acts otherwise, either from timidity or from being badly advised, will be obliged ever to be sword in hand, and will never be able to rely upon his subjects, who in turn will not be able to rely upon him, because of the constant fresh wrongs committed by him. Cruelties should be committed all at once, as in that way each separate one is less felt, and gives less offence; benefits, on the other hand, should be conferred one at a time, for in that way they will be more appreciated. But above all a prince should live upon such terms with his subjects that no accident, either for good or for evil, should make him vary his conduct toward them. For when adverse times bring upon you the necessity for action, you will no longer be in time to do evil; and the good you may do will not profit you, because it will be regarded as having been forced from you, and therefore will bring you no thanks.

CHAPTER IX

OF CIVIL PRINCIPALITIES

But let us come now to that other case, when a prominent citizen has become prince of his country, not by treason and violence, but by the favor of his fellow-citizens. This may be called a civil principality; and to attain it requires neither great courage and talent nor extraordinary good fortune, but rather a happy shrewdness. I say, then, that such principalities are achieved either by the favor of the people or by that of the nobles; for in every state there will be found two different dispositions, which result from the fact that the people dislike being ruled and oppressed by the nobles, while the nobles seek to rule and oppress the people. And this diversity of feeling and interests engenders one of three things: either a principality, or a government of liberty, or license. A principality results either from the will of the people or from that of the nobles, according as either the one or the other prevails and has the opportunity. For the nobles, seeing that they cannot resist the people, begin to have recourse to the influence and reputation of one of their own class, and make him a prince, so that under the shadow of his power they may give free scope to their desires. The people also, seeing that they cannot resist the nobles, have recourse to the influence and reputation of one man, and make him prince, so as to be protected by his authority. He who becomes prince by the aid of the nobles will have more difficulty in maintaining himself than he who arrives at that high station by the aid of the people. For the former finds himself surrounded by many who in their own opinion are equal to him, and for that reason he can neither command nor manage them in his own way. But he who attains the principality by favor of the people stands alone, and has around him none, or very few, that will not yield him a ready obedience. Moreover, you cannot satisfy the nobles with honesty, and without wrong to others, but it is easy to satisfy the people, whose aims are ever more honest than those of the nobles; the latter wishing to oppress, and the former being unwilling to be oppressed. I will say further, that a prince can never assure himself of a people who are hostile to him, for they are too numerous; the nobles on the other hand being but few, it becomes easy for a prince to make himself sure of them.

The worst that a prince may expect of a people who are unfriendly to him is that they will desert him; but the hostile nobles he has to fear, not only lest they abandon him, but also because they will turn against him. For they, being more farsighted and astute, always save themselves in advance, and seek to secure the favor of him whom they hope may be successful. The prince also is obliged always to live with the same people; but he can do very well without the same nobles, whom he can make and unmake at will any day, and bestow upon them or deprive them of their rank whenever it pleases him. The better to elucidate this subject, we must consider the nobles mainly in two ways; that is to say, they either shape their conduct so as to ally themselves entirely to your fortunes, or they do not. Those who attach themselves to you thus, if they are not rapacious, are to be honored and loved. Those who do not attach themselves to you must be regarded in two ways. Either they are influenced by pusillanimity and a natural lack of courage, and then you may make use of them, and especially of such as are men of intelligence; for in prosperity they will honor you, and in adversity you need not fear them. But if they purposely avoid attaching themselves to you from notions of ambition, then it is an evidence that they think more of their own interests than of yours; and of such men a prince must beware, and look upon them as open enemies, for when adversity comes they will always turn against him and contribute to his ruin.

Any one, therefore, who has become a prince by the favor of the people, must endeavor to preserve their good will, which will be easy for him, as they will ask of him no more than that he shall not oppress them. But he who, contrary to the will of the people, has become prince by the favor of the nobles, should at once and before everything else strive to win the good will of the people, which will be easy for him, by taking them under his protection. And as men, when they receive benefits from one of whom they expected only ill treatment, will attach themselves readily to such a benefactor, so the people will become more kindly disposed to such a one than if he had been made prince by their favor. Now a prince can secure the good will of the people in various ways, which differ with their character, and for which no fixed rules can be given. I will merely conclude by saying that it is essential for a prince to possess the good will and affection of his people, otherwise he will be utterly without support in time of adversity. Nabis, prince of Sparta, sustained the attacks of all Greece, and of a victorious Roman army, and successfully defended his country and his state against them; and when danger came, it was enough for him to be assured of a few supporters, which would not have sufficed if the people had been hostile to him. And let no one contravene this opinion of mine by quoting the trite saying, that "he who relies upon the people builds upon quicksand"; though this may be true when a private citizen places his reliance upon the people in the belief that they will come to his relief when he is oppressed by his enemies or the magistrates. In such a case he will often find himself deceived; as happened in Rome to the Gracchi, and in Florence to Messer Scali. But it being a prince who places his reliance upon those whom he might command, and being a man of courage and undismayed by adversity, and not having neglected to make proper preparations, and keeping all animated by his own courageous example and by his orders, he will not be deceived by the people; and it will be seen that the foundations of his state are laid solidly.

Those princes run great risks who attempt to change a civil government into an absolute one; for such princes command either in person or by means of magistrates. In the latter case, their state is more feeble and precarious; for the prince is in all things dependent upon the will of those citizens who are placed at the head of the magistracy, who, particularly in times of adversity, may with great ease deprive him of the government, either by open opposition or by refusing him obedience. For when danger is upon him, the prince is no longer in time to assume absolute authority; for the citizens and subjects who have been accustomed to receive their commands from the magistrates will not be disposed to yield obedience to the prince when in adversity. Thus in doubtful times there will ever be a lack of men whom he can trust. Such a prince cannot depend upon what he observes in ordinary quiet times, when the citizens have need of his authority; for then everybody runs at his bidding, everybody promises, and everybody is willing to die for him, when death is very remote. But in adverse times, when the government has need of the citizens, then but few will be found to stand by the prince. And this experience is the more dangerous as it can only be made once.

A wise prince, therefore, will steadily pursue such a course that the citizens of his state will always and under all circumstances feel the need of his authority, and will therefore always prove faithful to him.

CHAPTER X

IN WHAT MANNER THE POWER OF ALL PRINCIPALITIES SHOULD BE MEASURED

In examining the nature of the different principalities, it is proper to consider another point; namely, whether a prince is sufficiently powerful to be able, in case of need, to sustain himself, or whether he is obliged always to depend upon others for his defense. And to explain this point the better, I say that, in my judgment, those are able to maintain themselves who, from an abundance of men and money, can put a well-appointed army into the field, and meet any one in open battle that may attempt to attack them. And I esteem those as having need of the constant support of others who cannot meet their enemies in the field, but are under the necessity of taking refuge behind walls and keeping within them. Of the first case I have already treated, and shall speak of it again hereafter as occasion may require. Of the second case I cannot say otherwise than that it behooves such princes to fortify the cities where they have their seat of government, and to provide them well with all necessary supplies, without paying much attention to the country. For any prince that has thoroughly fortified the city in which he resides, and has in other respects placed himself on a good footing with his subjects, as has been explained above, will not be readily attacked. For men will ever be indisposed to engage in enterprises that present manifest difficulties; and it cannot be regarded as an easy undertaking to attack a prince in a city which he has thoroughly fortified, and who is not hated by his people.

The cities of Germany enjoy great liberties; they own little land outside of the walls, and obey the Emperor at their pleasure, fearing neither him nor any other neighboring power; for they are so well fortified that their capture would manifestly be tedious and difficult. They all have suitable walls and ditches, and are amply supplied with artillery, and always keep in their public magazines a year's supply of provisions, drink, and fuel. Moreover, by way of feeding the people without expense to the public, they always keep on hand a common stock of raw materials to last for one year, so as to give employment in those branches of industry by which the people are accustomed to gain their living, and which are the nerve and life of the city. They also attach much importance to military exercises, and have established many regulations for their proper practice.

A prince, then, who has a well-fortified city, and has not made himself odious to his people, cannot be readily attacked; and if any one be nevertheless rash enough to make the attempt, he would have to abandon it ignominiously, for the things of this world are so uncertain that it seems almost impossible that any one should be able to remain a whole year with his army inactive, carrying on the siege.

And if any one were to argue that, if the people who have possessions outside of the city were to see them ravaged and destroyed by the enemy, they would lose their patience, and that their selfish desire to protect their property would cause them to forget their attachment to the prince, I would meet this objection by saying, that a powerful and valiant prince will easily overcome this difficulty by encouraging his subjects with the hope that the evil will not endure long, or by alarming them with fears of the enemy's cruelty, or by assuring himself adroitly of those who have been too forward in expressing their discontent.

It is, moreover, reasonable to suppose that the enemy will ravage and destroy the country immediately upon his arrival before the city, and while its inhabitants are still full of courage and eager for defense. The prince, therefore, has the less ground for apprehension, because, by the time that the ardor of his people has cooled somewhat, the damage has already been done, and the evil is past remedy. And then the people will be the more ready to stand by their prince, for they will regard him as under obligations to them, their houses having been burned and their property ravaged in his defense. For it is the nature of mankind to become as much attached to others by the benefits which they bestow on them, as by those which they receive.

All things considered, then, it will not be difficult for a prudent prince to keep up the courage of his citizens in time of siege, both in the beginning as well as afterward, provided there be no lack of provisions or means of defense.

CHAPTER XI

OF ECCLESIASTICAL PRINCIPALITIES

It remains now only to speak of ecclesiastical principalities, in the attainment of which all difficulties occur beforehand. To achieve them requires either courage and talent or good fortune; but they are maintained without either the one or the other, for they are sustained by the ancient ordinances of religion, which are so powerful and of such quality that they maintain their princes in their position, no matter what their conduct or mode of life may be. These are the only princes that have states without the necessity of defending them, and subjects without governing them; and their states, though undefended, are not taken from them, while their subjects are indifferent to the fact that they are not governed, and have no thought of the possibility of alienating themselves from their princes.

These ecclesiastical principalities, then, are the only ones that are secure and happy; and being under the direction of that supreme wisdom to which human minds cannot attain, I will abstain from all further discussion of them; for they are raised up and sustained by the Divine Power, and it would be a bold and presumptuous office for any man to discuss them.

Nevertheless, if any one asks how it comes that the Church has acquired such power and greatness in temporal matters, while previous to Alexander VI all the Italian potentates, and even the great barons and the smallest nobles, paid so little regard to the temporal power of the Church, while now a King of France trembles before it, and this power has been able to drive him out of Italy and to ruin the Venetians, I shall not deem it superfluous to recall to memory the circumstances of the growth of this temporal power, although they are well known.

Before King Charles VIII of France came into Italy, that country was under the rule of the Pope, the Venetians, the King of Naples, the Duke of Milan, and the Florentines. These powers were obliged always to keep in view two important points: the one, not to permit any foreign power to come into Italy with an armed force; and the other, to prevent each other from further aggrandizement.

Those who had to be most closely watched by the others were the Pope and the Venetians. To restrain the latter required the united power of all the others, as was the case in the defense of Ferrara; and to keep the Pope in check they availed themselves of the barons of Rome, who were divided into two factions, the Orsini and the Colonna; there being constant cause of quarrel between them, they were always with arms in hand, under the very eyes of the Pope, which kept the papal power weak and infirm.

And although now and then a courageous Pope arose, who succeeded for a time in repressing these factions, as for instance Sixtus IV, yet neither wisdom nor good fortune could ever relieve them entirely from this annoyance. The cause of this difficulty was the shortness of their lives; for in the ten years which is about the average length of the life of a Pope, it would be difficult for him to crush out either one of these factions entirely. And if, for instance, one Pope should have succeeded in putting down the Colonna, another one, hostile to the Orsini, would arise and resuscitate the Colonna, but would not have the time to put down the Orsini. This was the reason why the temporal power of the Popes was so little respected in Italy.

Afterward Alexander VI came to the pontificate; he, more than any of his predecessors, showed what a Pope could accomplish with the money and power of the Church. Availing himself of the opportunity of the French invasion of Italy, and the instrumentality of the Duke Valentino, Alexander accomplished all those things which I have mentioned when speaking of the actions of the Duke. And although Alexander's object was not the aggrandizement of the Church, but rather that of his son, the Duke, yet all his efforts served to advance the interests of the Church, which, after his death and that of his son, fell heir to all the results of his labors.

Soon after came Julius II, who found the Church powerful, mistress of the entire Romagna, with the Roman barons crushed and the factions destroyed by the vigorous blows of Alexander. He also found the way prepared for the accumulation of money, which had never been employed before the time of Alexander. Julius II not only continued the system of Alexander, but carried it even further, and resolved to acquire the possession of Bologna, to ruin the Venetians, and to drive the French out of Italy, in all of which he succeeded. And this was the more praiseworthy in him, inasmuch as he did all these things, not for his own aggrandizement, but for that of the Church. He furthermore restrained the Orsini and the Colonna factions within the limits in which he found them upon his accession to the pontificate; and although there were some attempts at disturbances between them, yet there were two things that kept them down: one, the power of the Church, which overawed them; and the other, the fact that neither of them had any cardinals, who were generally the fomenters of the disturbances between them. Nor will these party feuds ever cease so long as the cardinals take any part in them. For it is they who stir up the factions in Rome as well as elsewhere, and then force the barons to sustain them. And it is thus that the ambition of these prelates gives rise to the discord and the disturbances among the barons.

His Holiness Pope Leo X thus found the Church allpowerful on his accession; and it is to be hoped that, if his predecessors have made the Church great by means of arms, he will make her still greater and more venerable by his goodness and his infinite other virtues.

CHAPTER XII

OF THE DIFFERENT KINDS OF TROOPS, AND OF MERCENARIES

Having discussed in detail the characteristics of all those kinds of principalities of which I proposed at the outset to treat, and having examined to some extent the causes of their success or failure, and explained the means by which many have sought to acquire and maintain them, it remains for me now to discuss generally the means of offense and defense which such princes may have to employ, under the various circumstances above referred to.

We have said how necessary it is for a prince to lay solid foundations for his power, as without such he would inevitably be ruined. The main foundations which all states must have, whether new, or old, or mixed, are good laws and good armies. And as there can be no good laws where there are not good armies, so the laws will be apt to be good where the armies are so. I will therefore leave the question of the laws, and confine myself to that of the armies. I say, then, that the armies with which a prince defends his state are either his own, or they are mercenaries or auxiliaries, or they are mixed. Mercenary and auxiliary troops are both useless and dangerous; and if any one attempts to found his state upon mercenaries, it will never be stable or secure; for they are disunited, ambitious, and without discipline,—faithless, and braggarts among friends, but among enemies cowards, and have neither fear of God nor good faith with men; so that the ruin of the prince who depends on them will be deferred only just so long as attack is delayed; and in peace he will be spoliated by his mercenaries, and in war by his enemies. The reason of all this is, that mercenary troops are not influenced by affection, or by any other consideration except their small stipend, which is not enough to make them willing to die for you. They are ready to serve you as soldiers so long as you are at peace; but when war comes, they will either run away or march off. There is no difficulty in demonstrating the truth of this; for the present ruin of Italy can be attributed to nothing else but to the fact that she has for many years depended upon mercenary armies, who for a time had some success, and seemed brave enough among themselves, but so soon as a foreign enemy came they showed what stuff they were made of. This was the reason why Charles VIII, King of France, was allowed to take Italy with scarcely an effort, and as it were with merely a piece of chalk.[1] Those who assert that our misfortunes were caused by our own faults speak the truth; but these faults were not such as are generally supposed to have been the cause, but those rather which I have pointed out; and as it was the princes who committed these faults, so they also suffered the penalties.

I will demonstrate more fully the unhappy consequences of employing mercenary armies. Their commanders are

---

[1] This expression of taking Italy "as it were with merely a piece of chalk" (*col gesso*) was made use of by Alexander VI, and means that Charles VIII had merely to send a quartermaster ahead with "a piece of chalk" to mark the houses in which the French troops were to be quartered.

either competent, or they are not; if they are, then you cannot trust them, because their chief aim will always be their own aggrandizement, either by imposing upon you, who are their employer, or by oppressing others beyond your intentions; and if they are incompetent, then they will certainly hasten your ruin. If now you meet these remarks by saying that the same will be the case with every commander, whether of mercenary troops or others, I reply, that, inasmuch as armies are employed either by princes or by republics, the prince should always in person perform the duty of commanding his army, and a republic should send one of her own citizens to command her troops, and in case he should not be successful, then they must change him; but if he is victorious, then they must be careful to keep him within the law, so that he may not exceed his powers. Experience has shown that princes as well as republics achieve the greatest success in war when they themselves direct the movements of their own armies, while mercenary troops do nothing but damage; and that a republic that has armies of her own is much less easily subjected to servitude by one of her own citizens, than one that depends upon foreign troops.

Thus Rome and Sparta maintained their liberties for many centuries by having armies of their own; the Swiss are most thoroughly armed, and consequently enjoy the greatest independence and liberty. The Carthaginians, on the other hand, furnish an example of the danger of employing mercenaries, for they came very near being subjugated by them at the close of the first war with Rome, although they had appointed some of their own citizens as commanders. After the death of Epaminondas, the Thebans made Philip of Macedon commander of their army, who after having been victorious deprived the Thebans of their liberty. The Milanese, after the death of Duke Philip, employed Francesco Sforza against the Venetians; after having defeated them at Caravaggio, he combined with them to subjugate his employers, the Milanese. The father of Francesco Sforza, who was commander in the service of Queen Joanna of Naples, suddenly left her entirely without troops, in consequence of which she was compelled to throw herself upon the protection of the King of Aragon, to save her kingdom. And if the Venetians and the Florentines formerly extended their dominions by means of mercenaries, and without their commanders attempting to make themselves princes of the country, but rather defending it loyally, I can only say that the Florentines were greatly favored by fortune in that respect. For of the valiant captains whose ambition they might have feared, some were not victorious, some never met an enemy, and others directed their ambition elsewhere. Among those who were not victorious was Giovanni Aguto,[1] whose good faith was never put to the test, he having been unsuccessful in the field; although it will be generally admitted that, had he been successful, the Florentines would have been at his mercy. The Sforzas and the Bracceschi were always opposed to each other, which caused Francesco to direct his ambition toward Lombardy, while Braccio turned his toward the Church and the kingdom of Naples.

But let us come now to occurrences of more recent date. The Florentines had conferred the command of their troops upon Paolo Vitelli, a soldier of the greatest ability, who had risen from private station to the highest post and rep-

---

[1] John Sharpe, an English soldier of fortune.

utation. No one will deny that, if he had succeeded in taking Pisa, the Florentines would have been obliged to submit to him; for had he gone over to the enemy, they would have been helpless, and if they kept him they would have been obliged to submit to his terms.

If now we look at the Venetians, we shall find that they carried on their wars securely and gloriously so long as they confined themselves to their proper element, the water, where they conducted their operations most bravely with their nobles and their own people. But when they engaged in wars on land, they no longer acted with their customary bravery, and adopted the habit of the other Italian states of employing mercenary troops. And although at the beginning of the growth of their dominion on land they had no occasion to have any serious apprehensions of their commanders, because their own reputation was great and their possessions on land small, yet when they extended these, which was under the captaincy of Carmignuola, they became sensible of their error. For although they were aware that it was by his superior conduct that they had defeated the Duke of Milan, yet on observing his lukewarmness in the further conduct of the war, they concluded that they could no longer hope for victory under his command. Still they dared not dismiss him for fear of losing what they had gained, and therefore they deemed it necessary for their own security to put him to death.

After that, the Venetians employed as generals of their forces Bartolommeo da Bergamo, Ruberto da San Severino, the Count Pittigliano, and the like, with whom they had reason rather to apprehend losses than to expect successes; as indeed happened afterward at Vaila, where in one battle they lost what had taken them eight hundred years of great labor to acquire; for with this kind of troops acquisitions are feeble and slow, while losses are quick and extraordinary.

Having thus far confined my examples to Italy, which has been for many years controlled by mercenary armies, I will now go back to an earlier period in discussing this subject; so that, having seen the origin and progress of the system, it may be the more effectually corrected. You must know, then, that in the earlier times, so soon as the Roman Empire began to lose its power and credit in Italy, and when the Pope acquired more influence in temporal matters, Italy became subdivided into a number of states. Many of the large cities took up arms against their nobles, who, encouraged by the Emperor, had kept them oppressed. The Church, by way of increasing her own influence in temporal matters, favored this revolt of the cities against their nobles. In many other cities the supreme power was usurped by some of their own citizens, who made themselves princes of the same. Thus it was that Italy, as it were, passed under the dominion of the Church and certain republics. And as these citizens and prelates were not accustomed to the management of armies, they began to hire foreigners for this purpose. The first who brought this sort of military into high repute was Alberigo da Como, a native of the Romagna. It was under his discipline that Braccio and Sforza were trained, and these in turn became the arbiters of Italy. They were succeeded by all those others who up to our time have led the armies of Italy; and the result of all their valor was that she was overrun by the French under Charles VIII, ravaged and plundered by Louis XII, oppressed by Ferdinand of Spain, and insulted and vituperated by the Swiss.

The course which these mercenary leaders pursued for the purpose of giving reputation and credit to their own mounted forces was, first, to decry and destroy the reputation of the infantry of the several states. They did this because, having no territorial possessions of their own, and being mere soldiers of fortune, they could achieve no reputation by means of a small body of infantry, and for a larger force they could not furnish subsistence. And therefore they confined themselves to cavalry, a smaller force of which enabled them the more readily to gain success and credit, and was at the same time more easily subsisted. In this way they brought matters to that point, that in an army of twenty thousand there were not over two thousand infantry.

Moreover, they used all means and ingenuity to avoid exposing themselves and their men to great fatigue and danger, and never killing each other in their encounters, but merely taking prisoners, who were afterward liberated without ransom. They never make any night attacks when besieging a place, nor did the besieged make any night sorties; they never properly intrenched their camps, and never kept the field in winter. All these practices were permitted by their rules of war, which were devised by them expressly, as we have said, to avoid hardships and danger; so that Italy was brought to shame and slavery by this system of employing mercenary troops.

CHAPTER XIII

OF AUXILIARIES, AND OF MIXED AND NATIONAL TROOPS

Auxiliary troops, which are the other kind which I have characterized in the preceding chapter as useless, are such as are furnished by a powerful ally whom a prince calls upon to come with his troops to aid and defend him; as was done quite lately by Pope Julius II, who, having had sad proof of the inefficiency of mercenaries in his attempt upon Ferrara, resorted to auxiliaries, and arranged with Ferdinand of Spain to send his armies to his assistance.

Troops of this kind may be useful and good in themselves, but they are always dangerous for him who calls them to his aid; for if defeated, he remains undone, and if victorious, then he is in their power like a prisoner. And although I could adduce numerous examples of this from ancient history, yet I will here cite that of Pope Julius II, which is still fresh in our minds, and whose conduct in that respect could not well have been more imprudent than what it was. For, wishing to take Ferrara, he placed himself in the hands of a foreigner. Fortunately for him, however, an incident occurred which saved him from the full effect of his bad selection; for his auxiliaries having been defeated at Ravenna, the Swiss suddenly appeared on the field and put the victors to ignominious flight. And thus Julius II escaped becoming prisoner either to his enemies who had fled, or to his auxiliaries; for the enemy's defeat was not due to their assistance, but to that of others.

The Florentines, having no army of their own, and wishing to get possession of Pisa, employed for that purpose ten thousand French troops, and were involved in greater danger by them than they had ever experienced from any other difficulty. The Emperor of Constantinople, by way of resisting the attacks of his neighbors, put ten thousand troops into Greece, who at the termination of the war refused to leave the country again; and this was the beginning of the subjection of Greece to the infidels.

Whoever, then, desires not to be victorious, let him employ auxiliary troops, for they are much more dangerous even than mercenaries. For your ruin is certain with auxiliaries, who are all united in their obedience to another; while mercenaries, even after victory, need more time and greater opportunity to injure you, for they are not one homogeneous body, and have been selected by yourself and are in your pay, and their commander being appointed by you, he cannot so quickly gain sufficient influence over these troops to enable him to injure you. In short, with mercenaries the danger lies in their cowardice and bad faith; while with auxiliaries their valor constitutes the danger.

A wise prince, therefore, should ever avoid employing either one of them, and should rely exclusively upon his own troops, and should prefer defeat with them rather than victory with the troops of others, with whom no real victory can ever be won. In proof of this, I shall not hesitate again to cite the conduct of Cesare Borgia. This Duke entered the Romagna with auxiliaries, taking there only

French troops, with whom he took Imola and Furli. But thinking afterward that these troops were not reliable, he had recourse to mercenaries, whom he deemed less dangerous, and engaged the Orsini and the Vitelli. These, however, proved themselves by their conduct to be uncertain, faithless, and dangerous; and therefore the Duke destroyed them, and then relied upon his own troops exclusively. The difference between the one and the other of these troops is easily seen when we look at the reputation of the Duke Valentino at the time when he employed the Orsini and the Vitelli, and when he had none but his own troops; for then his credit increased steadily, and the Duke was never more highly esteemed than when every one saw that he was thoroughly master of his armies.

I did not intend to depart from Italian and recent instances, and yet I cannot leave unnoticed the case of Hiero of Syracuse, being one of those to whom I have referred before. Having been made general of the Syracusan army, as before stated, he quickly perceived that mercenary troops were not useful, their commanders being appointed in a similar manner as our Italian Condottieri. And as it seemed to Hiero that he could neither keep nor dismiss them with safety, he had them all put to death and cut to pieces, and thenceforth carried on the war exclusively with troops of his own.

I will also recall to memory an illustration from the Old Testament applicable to this subject. David having offered to go and fight the Philistine bully, Goliath, Saul, by way of encouraging David, gave him his own arms and armor, which David however declined, after having tried them, saying that he could not make the most of his strength if he used those arms; and therefore he preferred to meet the enemy with no other arms but his sling and his knife. In short, the armor of another never suits you entirely; it is either too large and falls off your back, or weighs you down, or it is too tight.

Charles VII, father of Louis XI, King of France, having by his valor and good fortune delivered France from the English, recognized the necessity of depending solely upon his own armies, and organized in his kingdom regular companies of artillery, cavalry, and infantry. His son, Louis XI, afterward disbanded the infantry, and began to hire Swiss soldiers in their stead. This error, being followed by others, is now seen to have been the cause of the dangers to which that kingdom was exposed; for by giving prominence to the Swiss, Louis depreciated his own troops, and having disbanded his own infantry entirely, and accustomed his mounted forces to the support of the Swiss, they felt that they could have no success without them. Thence it came that the French could not hold their own against the Swiss, and without their support they could not stand against others. And thus the French armies have remained mixed, that is to say, partly their own troops and partly mercenaries; which, although better than either auxiliaries or mercenaries alone, yet makes them much worse than if they were composed exclusively of their own troops. Let this example suffice; for the kingdom of France would have been invincible if the military system established by Charles VII had been persevered in and extended. But the short-sightedness of men leads them to adopt any measure that for the moment seems good, and which does not openly reveal the poison concealed under it, as I have said above of hectic fevers.

A prince, then, who does not promptly recognize evils as they arise, cannot be called wise; but unfortunately this faculty is given to but few. And if we reflect upon the beginning of the ruin of the Roman Empire, it will be found to have resulted solely from hiring the Goths for its armies; for that was the first cause of the enervation of the forces of the Empire; and the valor of which the Romans divested themselves was thus transferred to the Goths.

I conclude, then, that no prince can ever be secure that has not an army of his own; and he will become wholly dependent upon fortune if in times of adversity he lacks the valor to defend himself. And wise men have ever held the opinion, that nothing is more weak and unstable than the reputation of power when not founded upon forces of the prince's own; by which I mean armies composed of his own subjects or citizens, or of his own creation;—all others are either mercenaries or auxiliaries.

The means for organizing such armies of his own will readily be found by the prince by studying the method in which Philip of Macedon, father of Alexander the Great, and many republics and princes, organized their armies, to which I refer in all respects.

CHAPTER XIV

*OF THE DUTIES OF A PRINCE IN RELATION
TO MILITARY MATTERS*

A prince, then, should have no other thought or object so much at heart, and make no other thing so much his special study, as the art of war and the organization and discipline of his army; for that is the only art that is expected of him who commands. And such is its power, that it not only maintains in their position those who were born princes, but it often enables men born in private station to achieve the rank of princes. And on the other hand, we have seen that princes who thought more of indulgence in pleasure than of arms have thereby lost their states.

Thus the neglect of the art of war is the principal cause of the loss of your state, while a proficiency in it often enables you to acquire one. Francesco Sforza, from being skilled in arms, rose from private station to be Duke of Milan; and his descendants, by shunning the labors and fatigue of arms, relapsed into the condition of private citizens.

Among the other causes of evil that will befall a prince who is destitute of a proper military force is, that it will cause him to be scorned; which is one of those disgraces against which a prince ought specially to guard, as we shall demonstrate further on. For there is no sort of proportion between one who is well armed and one who is not so; nor is it reasonable that he who is armed should voluntarily obey the unarmed, or that a prince who is without a military force should remain secure among his armed subjects. For when there is disdain on the one side and mistrust on the other, it is impossible that the two should work well together. A prince, then, who is not master of the art of war, besides other misfortunes, cannot be respected by his soldiers, nor can he depend upon them. And therefore should the practice of arms ever be uppermost in the prince's thoughts; he should study it in time of peace as much as in actual war, which he can do in two ways, the one by practical exercise, and the other by scientific study. As regards the former, he must not only keep his troops well disciplined and exercised, but he must also frequently follow the chase, whereby his body will become inured to hardships, and he will become familiar with the character of the country, and learn where the mountains rise and the valleys debouch, and how the plains lie; he will learn to know the nature of rivers and of the swamps, to all of which he should give the greatest attention. For this knowledge is valuable in many ways to the prince, who thereby learns to know his own country, and can therefore better understand its defense. Again, by the knowledge of and practical acquaintance with one country, he will with greater facility comprehend the character of others, which it may be necessary for him to understand. For instance, the mountains, valleys, plains, rivers, and swamps of Tuscany bear a certain resemblance to those of other provinces; so that by the knowledge of the character and formation of one country he will readily arrive at that of others. A prince who is wanting in that experience lacks the very first essentials which a commander should possess; for that knowledge teaches him where to find the enemy, to select proper places for intrenchments, to conduct armies, regulate marches, and order battles, and to keep the field with advantage.

Among other praises that have been accorded by different writers to Philopœmen, prince of the Achaians, was, that in time of peace he devoted himself constantly to the study of the art of war; and when he walked in the country with friends, he often stopped and argued with them thus: "Suppose the enemy were on yonder mountain, and we should happen to be here with our army, which of the two would have the advantage? How could we go most safely to find the enemy, observing proper order? If we should wish to retreat, how should we proceed? And if the enemy were to retreat, which way had we best pursue him?" And thus in walking he proposed to his friends all the cases that possibly could occur with an army, hearing their opinions, and giving his own, and corroborating them with reasons; so that by these continued discussions no case could ever arise in the conduct of an army for which he had not thought of the proper remedy. As regards the exercise of the mind, the prince should read history, and therein study the actions of eminent men, observe how they bore themselves in war, and examine the causes of their victories and defeats, so that he may imitate the former and avoid the latter. But above all should he follow the example of whatever distinguished man he may have chosen for his model; assuming that some one has been specially praised and held up to him as glorious, whose actions and exploits he should ever bear in mind. Thus it is told of Alexander that he imitated Achilles, and of Cæsar that he had taken Alexander for his model, as Scipio had done with Cyrus. And whoever reads the life of Cyrus, written by Xenophon, will not fail to recognize afterward, in the life of Scipio, of how much value this imitation was to him, and how closely the latter conformed in point of temperance, affability, humanity, and liberality to the accounts given of Cyrus by Xenophon.

A wise prince then should act in like manner, and should never be idle in times of peace, but should industriously lay up stores of which to avail himself in times of adversity; so that, when Fortune abandons him, he may be prepared to resist her blows.

CHAPTER XV

OF THE MEANS BY WHICH MEN, AND ESPECIALLY PRINCES, WIN APPLAUSE, OR INCUR CENSURE

It remains now to be seen in what manner a prince should conduct himself toward his subjects and his allies; and knowing that this matter has already been treated by many others, I apprehend that my writing upon it also may be deemed presumptuous, especially as in the discussion of the same I shall differ from the rules laid down by others. But as my aim is to write something that may be useful to him for whom it is intended, it seems to me proper to pursue the real truth of the matter, rather than to indulge in mere speculation on the same; for many have imagined republics and principalities such as have never been known to exist in reality. For the manner in which men live is so different from the way in which they ought to live, that he who leaves the common course for that which he ought to follow will find that it leads him to ruin rather than to safety. For a man who, in all respects, will carry out only his professions of good, will be apt to be ruined among so many who are evil. A prince therefore who desires to maintain himself must learn to be not always good, but to be so or not as necessity may require. Leaving aside then the imaginary things concerning princes, and confining ourselves only to the realities, I say that all men when they are spoken of, and more especially princes, from being in a more conspicuous position, are noted for some quality that brings them either praise or censure. Thus one is deemed liberal, another miserly (*misero*) to use a Tuscan expression (for avaricious is he who by rapine desires to gain, and miserly we call him who abstains too much from the enjoyment of his own). One man is esteemed generous, another rapacious; one cruel, another merciful; one faithless, and another faithful; one effeminate and pusillanimous, another ferocious and brave; one affable, another haughty; one lascivious, another chaste; one sincere, the other cunning; one facile, another inflexible; one grave, another frivolous; one religious, another sceptical; and so on.

I am well aware that it would be most praiseworthy for a prince to possess all of the above-named qualities that are esteemed good; but as he cannot have them all, nor entirely observe them, because of his human nature which does not permit it, he should at least be prudent enough to know how to avoid the infamy of those vices that would rob him of his state; and if possible also to guard against such as are likely to endanger it. But if that be not possible, then he may with less hesitation follow his natural inclinations. Nor need he care about incurring censure for such vices, without which the preservation of his state may be difficult. For, all things considered, it will be found that some things that seem like virtue will lead you to ruin if you follow them; while others, that apparently are vices, will, if followed, result in your safety and well-being.

CHAPTER XVI

OF LIBERALITY AND PARSIMONIOUSNESS

To begin with the first of the above-named qualities, I say that it is well for a prince to be deemed liberal; and yet liberality, indulged in so that you will no longer be feared, will prove injurious. For liberality worthily exercised, as it should be, will not be recognized, and may bring upon you the reproach of the very opposite. For if you desire the reputation of being liberal, you must not stop at any degree of sumptuousness; so that a prince will in this way generally consume his entire substance, and may in the end, if he wishes to keep up his reputation for liberality, be obliged to subject his people to extraordinary burdens, and resort to taxation, and employ all sorts of measures that will enable him to procure money. This will soon make him odious with his people; and when he becomes poor, he will be scorned by everybody; so that having by his prodigality injured many and benefited few, he will be the first to suffer every inconvenience, and be exposed to every danger. And when he becomes conscious of this and attempts to retrench, he will at once expose himself to the imputation of being a miser.

A prince then, being unable without injury to himself to practice the virtue of liberality in such manner that it may be generally recognized, should not, when he becomes aware of this and is prudent, mind incurring the charge of parsimoniousness. For after a while, when it is seen that by his prudence and economy he makes his revenues suffice him, and that he is able to provide for his defense in case of war, and engage in enterprises without burdening his people, he will be considered liberal enough by all those from whom he takes nothing, and these are the many; while only those to whom he does not give, and which are the few, will look upon him as parsimonious.

In our own times we have not seen any great things accomplished except by those who were regarded as parsimonious; all others have been ruined. Pope Julius II, having been helped by his reputation of liberality to attain the pontificate, did not afterward care to keep up that reputation to enable him to engage in war against the King of France; and he carried on ever so many wars without levying any extraordinary taxes. For his long-continued economy enabled him to supply the extraordinary expenses of his wars.

If the present King of Spain had sought the reputation of being liberal, he would not have been able to engage in so many enterprises, nor could he have carried them to a successful issue. A prince, then, who would avoid robbing his own subjects, and be able to defend himself, and who would avoid becoming poor and abject or rapacious, should not mind incurring the reputation of being parsimonious; for that is one of those vices that will enable him to maintain his state. And should it be alleged that Julius Cæsar attained the Empire by means of his liberality, and that many others by the same reputation have achieved the highest rank, then I reply, that you are either already a prince, or are in the way of becoming one; in the first case liberality would be injurious to you, but in the second it certainly is necessary to be reputed liberal. Now Cæsar was aiming to attain the Empire of Rome; but having achieved it, had he lived and not moderated his expenditures, he would assuredly have ruined the Empire by his prodigality.

And were any one to assert that there have been many princes who have achieved great things with their armies, and who were accounted most liberal, I answer that a prince either spends his own substance and that of his subjects, or that of others. Of the first two he should be very sparing, but in spending that of others he ought not to omit any act of liberality. The prince who in person leads his armies into foreign countries, and supports them by plunder, pillage, and exactions, and thus dispenses the substance of others, should do so with the greatest liberality, as otherwise his soldiers would not follow him. For that which belongs neither to him nor to his own subjects, a prince may spend most lavishly, as was done by Cyrus, Cæsar, and Alexander. The spending of other people's substance will not diminish, but rather increase, his reputation; it is only the spending of his own that is injurious to a prince.

And there is nothing that consumes itself so quickly as liberality; for the very act of using it causes it to lose the faculty of being used, and will either impoverish you and make you despised, or it will make you rapacious and odious. And of all the things against which a prince should guard most carefully is incurring the hatred and contempt of his subjects. Now, liberality will bring upon you either the one or the other; there is therefore more wisdom in submitting to be called parsimonious, which may bring you blame without hatred, than, by aiming to be called liberal, to incur unavoidably the reputation of rapacity, which will bring upon you infamy as well as hatred.

CHAPTER XVII

OF CRUELTY AND CLEMENCY, AND WHETHER IT IS BETTER TO BE LOVED THAN FEARED

Coming down now to the other aforementioned qualities, I say that every prince ought to desire the reputation of being merciful, and not cruel; at the same time, he should be careful not to misuse that mercy. Cesare Borgia was reputed cruel, yet by his cruelty he reunited the Romagna to his states, and restored that province to order, peace, and loyalty; and if we carefully examine his course, we shall find it to have been really much more merciful than the course of the people of Florence, who, to escape the reputation of cruelty, allowed Pistoia to be destroyed. A prince, therefore, should not mind the ill repute of cruelty, when he can thereby keep his subjects united and loyal; for a few displays of severity will really be more merciful than to allow, by an excess of clemency, disorders to occur, which are apt to result in rapine and murder; for these injure a whole community, while the executions ordered by the prince fall only upon a few individuals. And, above all others, the new prince will find it almost impossible to avoid the reputation of cruelty, because new states are generally exposed to many dangers. It was on this account that Virgil made Dido to excuse the severity of her government, because it was still new, saying,—

"Res dura, et regni novitas me talia cogunt
    Moliri, et late fines custode tueri."[1]

A prince, however, should be slow to believe and to act; nor should he be too easily alarmed by his own fears, and should proceed moderately and with prudence and humanity, so that an excess of confidence may not make him incautious, nor too much mistrust make him intolerant. This, then, gives rise to the question "whether it be better to be beloved than feared, or to be feared than beloved." It will naturally be answered that it would be desirable to be both the one and the other; but as it is difficult to be both at the same time, it is much more safe to be feared than to be loved, when you have to choose between the two. For

---

[1] "My cruel fate,
And doubts attending an unsettled state,
Force me to guard my coasts from foreign foes."
                                    —DRYDEN.

it may be said of men in general that they are ungrateful and fickle, dissemblers, avoiders of danger, and greedy of gain. So long as you shower benefits upon them, they are all yours; they offer you their blood, their substance, their lives, and their children, provided the necessity for it is far off; but when it is near at hand, then they revolt. And the prince who relies upon their words, without having otherwise provided for his security, is ruined; for friendships that are won by rewards, and not by greatness and nobility of soul, although deserved, yet are not real, and cannot be depended upon in time of adversity.

Besides, men have less hesitation in offending one who makes himself beloved than one who makes himself feared; for love holds by a bond of obligation which, as mankind is bad, is broken on every occasion whenever it is for the interest of the obliged party to break it. But fear holds by the apprehension of punishment, which never leaves men. A prince, however, should make himself feared in such a manner that, if he has not won the affections of his people, he shall at least not incur their hatred; for the being feared, and not hated, can go very well together, if the prince abstains from taking the substance of his subjects, and leaves them their women. And if you should be obliged to inflict capital punishment upon any one, then be sure to do so only when there is manifest cause and proper justification for it; and, above all things, abstain from taking people's property, for men will sooner forget the death of their fathers than the loss of their patrimony. Besides, there will never be any lack of reasons for taking people's property; and a prince who once begins to live by rapine will ever find excuses for seizing other people's property. On the other hand, reasons for taking life are not so easily found, and are more readily exhausted. But when a prince is at the head of his army, with a multitude of soldiers under his command, then it is above all things necessary for him to disregard the reputation of cruelty; for without such severity an army cannot be kept together, nor disposed for any successful feat of arms.

Among the many admirable qualities of Hannibal, it is related of him that, having an immense army composed of a very great variety of races of men, which he led to war in foreign countries, no quarrels ever occurred among them, nor were there ever any dissensions between them and their chief, either in his good or in his adverse fortunes; which can only be accounted for by his extreme cruelty. This, together with his boundless courage, made him ever venerated and terrible in the eyes of his soldiers; and without that extreme severity all his other virtues would not have sufficed to produce that result.

Inconsiderate writers have, on the one hand, admired his great deeds, and, on the other, condemned the principal cause of the same. And the proof that his other virtues would not have sufficed him may be seen from the case of Scipio, who was one of the most remarkable men, not only of his own time, but in all history. His armies revolted in Spain solely in consequence of his extreme clemency, which allowed his soldiers more license than comports with proper military discipline. This fact was censured in the Roman Senate by Fabius Maximus, who called Scipio the corrupter of the Roman soldiers. The tribe of the Locrians having been wantonly destroyed by one of the lieutenants of Scipio, he neither punished him for that nor for his insolence,—simply because of his own easy nature; so that, when somebody wished to excuse Scipio in the Senate, he said, "that there were many men who knew better how to avoid errors themselves than to punish them in others." This easy nature of Scipio's would in time have dimmed his fame and glory if he had persevered in it under the Empire; but living as he did under the government of the Senate, this dangerous quality of his was not only covered up, but actually redounded to his honor.

To come back now to the question whether it be better to be beloved than feared, I conclude that, as men love of their own free will, but are inspired with fear by the will of the prince, a wise prince should always rely upon himself, and not upon the will of others; but, above all, should he always strive to avoid being hated, as I have already said above.

CHAPTER XVIII

IN WHAT MANNER PRINCES SHOULD KEEP THEIR FAITH

It must be evident to every one that it is more praiseworthy for a prince always to maintain good faith, and practice integrity rather than craft and deceit. And yet the experience of our own times has shown that those princes have achieved great things who made small account of good faith, and who understood by cunning to circumvent the intelligence of others; and that in the end they got the better of those whose actions were dictated by loyalty and good faith. You must know, therefore, that there are two ways of carrying on a contest; the one by law, and the other by force. The first is practiced by men, and the other by animals; and as the first is often insufficient, it becomes necessary to resort to the second.

A prince then should know how to employ the nature of man, and that of the beasts as well. This was figuratively taught by ancient writers, who relate how Achilles and many other princes were given to Chiron the centaur to be nurtured, and how they were trained under his tutorship; which fable means nothing else than that their preceptor combined the qualities of the man and the beast; and that a prince, to succeed, will have to employ both the one and the other nature, as the one without the other cannot produce lasting results.

It being necessary then for a prince to know well how to employ the nature of the beasts, he should be able to assume both that of the fox and that of the lion; for while the latter cannot escape the traps laid for him, the former cannot defend himself against the wolves. A prince should be a fox, to know the traps and snares; and a lion, to be able to frighten the wolves; for those who simply hold to the nature of the lion do not understand their business.

A sagacious prince then cannot and should not fulfill his pledges when their observance is contrary to his interest, and when the causes that induced him to pledge his faith no longer exist. If men were all good, then indeed this precept would be bad; but as men are naturally bad, and will not observe their faith toward you, you must, in the same way, not observe yours to them; and no prince ever yet lacked legitimate reasons with which to color his want of good faith. Innumerable modern examples could be given of this; and it could easily be shown how many treaties of peace, and how many engagements, have been made null and void by the faithlessness of princes; and he who has best known how to play the fox has ever been the most successful.

But it is necessary that the prince should know how to color this nature well, and how to be a great hypocrite and dissembler. For men are so simple, and yield so much to immediate necessity, that the deceiver will never lack dupes. I will mention one of the most recent examples. Alexander VI never did nor ever thought of anything but to deceive, and always found a reason for doing so. No one ever had greater skill in pledging his word, no one affirmed his pledges with greater oaths, and observed them less, than Pope Alexander; and yet he was always successful in his deceits, because he knew the weakness of men in that particular.

It is not necessary, however, for a prince to possess all the above-mentioned qualities; but it is essential that he should at least seem to have them. I will even venture to say, that to have and to practice them constantly is pernicious, but to seem to have them is useful. For instance, a prince should seem to be merciful, faithful, humane, religious, and upright, and should even be so in reality; but he should have his mind so trained that, when occasion requires it, he may know how to change to the opposite. And it must be understood that a prince, and especially one who has but recently acquired his state, cannot perform all those things which cause men to be esteemed as good; he being often obliged, for the sake of maintaining his state, to act contrary to humanity, charity, and religion. And therefore is it necessary that he should have a versatile mind, capable of changing readily, according as the winds and changes of fortune bid him; and, as has been said above, not to swerve from the good if possible, but to know how to resort to evil if necessity demands it.

A prince then should be very careful never to allow anything to escape his lips that does not abound in the above-named five qualities, so that to see and to hear him he may seem all charity, integrity, and humanity, all uprightness, and all piety. And more than all else is it necessary for a prince to seem to possess the last quality; for mankind in general judge more by what they see than by what they feel, every one being capable of the former, and but few of the latter. Everybody sees what you seem to be, but few really feel what you are; and these few dare not oppose the opinion of the many, who are protected by the majesty of the state; for the actions of all men, and especially those of princes, are judged by the result, where there is no other judge to whom to appeal.

A prince then should look mainly to winning, and to the successful maintenance of his state. The means which he employs for this will always be accounted honorable, and will be praised by everybody; for the common people are always taken by appearances and by results, and it is the vulgar mass that constitutes the world. But a very few have rank and station, while the many have nothing to sustain them. A certain prince of our time, whom it is well not to name, never preached anything but peace and good faith; but if he had always observed either the one or the other, it would in most instances have cost him his reputation or his state.

CHAPTER XIX

A PRINCE MUST AVOID BEING DESPISED AND HATED

Having thus considered separately the most important of the above-mentioned qualities which a prince should possess, I will now briefly discuss the others under this general maxim: that a prince should endeavor, as has already been said, to avoid everything that would tend to make him odious and despised. And in proportion as he avoids that will he have performed his part well, and need fear no danger from any other vices. Above all, a prince makes himself odious by rapacity, that is, by taking away from his subjects their property and their women, from which he should carefully abstain. The great mass of men will live quietly and contentedly, provided you do not rob them of their substance and their honor; so that you will have to contend only with the ambition of a few, which is easily restrained in various ways.

A prince becomes despised when he incurs by his acts the reputation of being variable, inconstant, effeminate, pusillanimous, and irresolute; he should therefore guard

against this as against a dangerous rock, and should strive
to display in all his actions grandeur, courage, gravity, and
determination. And in judging the private causes of his
subjects, his decisions should be irrevocable. Thus will he
maintain himself in such esteem that no one will think of
deceiving or betraying him. The prince, who by his habitual conduct gives cause for such an opinion of himself,
will acquire so great a reputation that it will be difficult
to conspire against him, or to attack him; provided that
it be generally known that he is truly excellent, and revered by his subjects. For there are two things which
a prince has to fear: the one, attempts against him by his
own subjects; and the other, attacks from without by
powerful foreigners. Against the latter he will be able to
defend himself by good armies and good allies, and whoever has the one will not lack the other. And so long as his
external affairs are kept quiet, his internal security will not
be disturbed, unless it should be by a conspiracy. And
even if he were to be assailed from without, if he has a
well-organized army and has lived as he should have done,
he will always (unless he should give way himself) be able
to withstand any such attacks, as we have related was
done by Nabis, tyrant of Sparta. But even when at peace
externally, it nevertheless behooves the prince to be on his
guard, lest his subjects conspire against him secretly. He
will, however, be sufficiently secure against this, if he
avoids being hated and despised, and keeps his subjects
well satisfied with himself, which should ever be his aim,
as I have already explained above. Not to be hated nor
scorned by the mass of the people is one of the best safe-
guards for a prince against conspiracies; for conspirators

always believe that the death of the prince will be satisfactory to the people; but when they know that it will
rather offend than conciliate the people, they will not venture upon such a course, for the difficulties that surround
conspirators are infinite.

Experience proves that, although there have been many
conspiracies, yet but few have come to a good end; for he
who conspires cannot act alone, nor can he take any as-
sociates except such as he believes to be malcontents; and
so soon as you divulge your plans to a malcontent, you
furnish him the means wherewith to procure satisfaction.
For by denouncing it he may hope to derive great advantages for himself, seeing that such a course will insure him
those advantages, while the other is full of doubts and
dangers. He must indeed be a very rare friend of yours, or
an inveterate enemy of the prince, to observe good faith
and not to betray you.

But to reduce this matter to a few words, I say that on
the side of the conspirator there is nothing but fear,
jealousy, and apprehension of punishment; while the prince
has on his side the majesty of sovereignty, the laws, the
support of his friends and of the government, which protect him. And if to all this be added the popular good will,
it seems impossible that any one should be rash enough
to attempt a conspiracy against him. For ordinarily a conspirator has cause for apprehension only before the execution of his evil purpose; but in this case, having the people
for his enemies, he has also to fear the consequences after
the commission of the crime, and can look nowhere for
a refuge. Upon this point I might adduce innumerable examples, but will content myself with only one, which oc-

curred within the memory of our fathers. Messer Annibale Bentivogli, grandfather of the present Messer Annibale, being prince of Bologna, was murdered by the Canneschi, who had conspired against him, and there remained of his family one Messer Giovanni, who was still in his infancy. Immediately after the murder of Messer Annibale, the people rose and killed all the Canneschi. This was the consequence of the popularity which the Bentivogli enjoyed in those days in Bologna, and which went to that extent that after the death of Messer Annibale, when there remained not one of the family in Bologna capable of governing the state, the people received information that there was a Bentivogli in Florence who, until then, had been reputed the son of a blacksmith. They sent a deputation to him at Florence and conferred the government of the city upon him, which he exercised undisturbed until Messer Giovanni came to be of suitable age to assume it himself. I conclude, that a prince need apprehend but little from conspiracies, provided he possess the good will of his people, which is one of the most important points that a prince has to look to.

Among the well-organized and well-governed kingdoms of our time is that of France, which has a great many excellent institutions that secure the liberty and safety of the King. The most important of these is the Parliament, and its authority; for the founder of that kingdom knew the ambition and insolence of the nobles, and judged it necessary to put a bit into their mouths with which to curb them. He knew at the same time the hatred of the mass of the people toward the nobles, based upon their fears. Wishing to secure both, and yet unwilling to make this the special care of the King, so as to relieve him of the responsibility to the nobles of seeming to favor the people, and to the people of favoring the nobles, he instituted the Parliament to act as a judge, which might, without reference to the King, keep down the great, and favor the weak. Nor could there be a wiser system, or one that affords more security to the King and his realm.

We may also draw another notable conclusion from this, namely, that princes should devolve all matters of responsibility upon others, and take upon themselves only those of grace. I conclude then anew, that a prince should avoid at the same time making himself odious to his people. It may perhaps seem to many that, considering the life and death of many Roman Emperors, their example contradicts my opinions, seeing that some who have led most exemplary lives, and displayed most noble qualities of the soul, yet lost the Empire, or were even killed by their followers, who had conspired against them. I desire to meet this objection, and will therefore discuss the characters of some of those Emperors, showing that the causes of their ruin were not different from those adduced by me above; and I will present some considerations that are important to the student of the history of those times. In this I shall confine myself to those Emperors that succeeded one another from Marcus, the philosopher, to Maximinius; namely, Marcus, his son Commodus, Pertinax, Julian, Severus, Antoninus Caracalla his son, Macrinus, Heliogabalus, Alexander, and Maximinius.

And I must remark at the outset, that, where in other principalities the prince had to contend only with the ambition of the nobles and the insolence of the people, the Roman Emperors had to meet a third difficulty, in having to bear with the cruelty and cupidity of the soldiers, which were so great that they caused the ruin of many, because of the difficulty of satisfying at the same time both the soldiers and the people; for the people love quiet, and for that reason they revere princes who are modest, while the soldiers love a prince of military spirit, and who is cruel, haughty, and rapacious. And these qualities the prince must practice upon the people, so as to enable him to increase the pay of the soldiers, and to satisfy their avarice and cruelty. Whence it came that all those Emperors were ruined who had not, by their natural or acquired qualities, the necessary influence that would enable them to restrain at the same time the soldiers and the people. Most of them, therefore, and especially those who had but recently attained the sovereignty, knowing the difficulty of satisfying two such different dispositions, sought rather to satisfy the soldiers, and cared but little about oppressing and offending the people. And this course was unavoidable for them; for inasmuch as princes generally cannot prevent being hated by some, they ought first of all to strive not to be hated by the mass of the people; but failing in this, they should by all means endeavor to avoid being hated by the more powerful. And therefore those Emperors who, by reason of having but recently acquired the Empire, had need of extraordinary favors, attached themselves more readily to the soldiery than to the people; which, however, was advantageous to them or not only according as such Emperor knew how to maintain his ascendency over them. These were the reasons why Marcus, Pertinax, and Alexander, being all three men of modest lives, lovers of justice, enemies to cruelty, humane, and benevolent, came to a bad end, Marcus alone excepted, who lived and died much honored; but he had succeeded to the Empire by inheritance, and was not indebted for it either to the soldiers or to the favor of the people. He was, moreover, endowed with many virtues, which made him generally revered; and so long as he lived he always kept both the soldiery and the people within their proper bounds, and thus was neither hated nor despised. But Pertinax was made Emperor contrary to the will of the army, which, having been accustomed under Commodus to a life of unrestrained license, could not bear the orderly life to which Pertinax wished to constrain them. Having thus incurred their hatred, to which disrespect became added on account of his age, he was ruined at the very outset of his reign. And here I would observe that hatred may be caused by good as well as by evil works, and therefore (as I have said above) a prince who wants to preserve his state is often obliged not to be good; for when the mass of the people or of the soldiery, or of the nobles, whose support is necessary for him, is corrupt, then it becomes the interest of the prince to indulge and satisfy their humor; and it is under such circumstances that good works will be injurious to him. Let us come now to Alexander, who was so good that, among other merits, it was said of him that during the fourteen years of his reign not one person was put to death by him without regular judicial proceedings. But being regarded as effeminate, and as allowing himself to be governed by his mother, he fell into disrespect, and the soldiery conspired against him and killed him.

Discussing now, by way of the opposite extreme, the qualities of Commodus, Severus, Antoninus Caracalla, and Maximinius, we find them to have been most cruel and rapacious; and that, for the sake of keeping the soldiers satisfied, they did not hesitate to commit every kind of outrage upon the people; and that all of them, with exception of Septimus Severus, came to a bad end. The latter possessed such valor that, although he imposed heavy burdens upon the people, yet, by keeping the soldiers his friends, he was enabled to reign undisturbed and happily; for his bravery caused him to be so much admired by the soldiers and the people that the latter were in a manner stupefied and astounded by it, while it made the former respectful and satisfied.

And as the actions of Severus were really great, considering that he was a prince of but recent date, I will show how well he knew to play the part of the fox and of the lion, whose natures a prince should be able to imitate, as I have shown above. Severus, knowing the indolence of the Emperor Julian, persuaded the troops which he commanded in Slavonia that it would be proper for them to go to Rome to avenge the death of Pertinax, who had been killed by the Imperial Guard. Under this pretext, without showing that he aspired to the Empire, he moved the army to Rome, and was in Italy before it was known even that he had started. On his arrival in Rome the Senate, under the influence of fear, elected Severus Emperor, Julian having previously been slain.

After this beginning, Severus had yet two difficulties to overcome before he could make himself master of the entire state: the one in Asia, where Niger, commander of the army of the East, had himself proclaimed Emperor; and the other in the West, caused by Albinus, who also aspired to the Empire. Deeming it dangerous to declare himself openly the enemy of both, Severus resolved to attack Niger and to deceive Albinus; and therefore he wrote to the latter that, having been elected Emperor by the

Senate, he wished to share that dignity with him, and accordingly sent him the title of Cæsar, and accepted him as his colleague, by resolution of the Senate. Albinus received it all as truth; but after Severus had defeated and slain Niger, and quieted matters in the East, he returned to Rome and complained in the Senate that Albinus, little grateful for the benefits which he had bestowed upon him, had plotted treason and murder against him, and that therefore it was incumbent upon him to go and punish this ingratitude and treason. Severus thereupon went into France to seek Albinus, and deprived him of his state and his life.

If now we examine minutely the conduct of Severus, we shall find that he combined the ferocity of the lion with the cunning of the fox, and that he was feared and revered by every one, and was not hated by the army. Nor ought we to be surprised to find that, although a new man, he yet should have been able to maintain himself at the head of so great an empire; for his eminent reputation saved him always from incurring the hatred of the people, which his rapacity might otherwise have provoked.

Antoninus Caracalla, the son of Severus, was also a man possessed of eminent qualities and rare gifts, which made him admired by the people and acceptable to the soldiery. For he was a military man, capable of enduring every fatigue, despising the delicacies of the table and every other effeminacy, which made him beloved by all the army. But his ferocity and cruelty were so great and unprecedented that, having on several occasions caused a large number of the people of Rome to be put to death, and at another time nearly the entire population of Alexandria, he became odious to the whole world, and began to be feared even by his immediate attendants, and finally was killed by a centurion in the midst of his army. Whence we may observe that princes cannot always escape assassination when prompted by a resolute and determined spirit; for any man who himself despises death can always inflict it upon others. But as men of this sort are rare, princes need not be very apprehensive about them; they should, however, be most careful not to offend grievously any of those who serve their persons, or who are around and near them in the service of the state. It was in this respect that Caracalla erred, for he had contumeliously slain a brother of a centurion, whom he had also threatened repeatedly, and yet kept him as one of his bodyguard; which was a most reckless thing to do, and well calculated to prove ruinous to Antoninus Caracalla, as it finally did.

But we come now to Commodus, who might have kept the Empire with great ease, having inherited it as the son of Marcus Aurelius. All he had to do was to follow in the footsteps of his father, which would have satisfied both the people and the army. But being of a cruel and bestial nature, he began by entertaining the army and making it licentious, so as to enable him the more freely to indulge his rapacity upon the people. And on the other hand he made himself contemptible in the eyes of his soldiers, by disregarding his own dignity, and descending into the arena to combat with gladiators, and doing other disgraceful things wholly unworthy of the imperial majesty. Being thus hated by the people and despised by the army, a conspiracy was set on foot against him and he was killed.

It remains now for me to discuss the character of Maximinius. He was a most warlike man; and the army being tired of the effeminacy of Alexander Severus, of which I have spoken above, they elected Maximinius to the Empire after the death of Alexander. But he did not retain it very long, for two circumstances made him both odious and despised. One was his extremely low origin, having been a shepherd in Thracia (which was generally known, and caused him to be held in great contempt by every one), and the other was his delay, when elected Emperor, to go to Rome, there to take possession of the imperial throne. He had moreover earned the reputation of extreme cruelty, in consequence of the many acts of ferocity which he had committed through the agency of his prefects in Rome and elsewhere. Being thus despised by the whole world on account of his low origin, and on the other hand hated because of his cruelty, a conspiracy was formed against him, first in Africa, and then by the Senate and people of Rome and all Italy. His army joined in the conspiracy, for being engaged in the siege of Aquileia and finding difficulty in taking it, they became tired of his harshness; and seeing that he had so many enemies, they lost their fear of him and put him to death.

I care not to discuss either Heliogabalus, or Macrinus, or Julian, who, being utterly contemptible, came quickly to an end; but will conclude this discourse by saying that the princes of our times are not subjected to the same difficulties in their governments by the extraordinary demands of their armies. For although they are obliged to show them some consideration, yet they are easily disposed of, as none of the sovereigns of the present day keep their armies constantly together, so as to become veterans in the service of the government and the administration of the provinces, as was the case in the time of the Roman Empire. And if in those days it was necessary to have more regard to the armies than to the people, because of their greater power, it nowadays behooves princes rather to keep the people contented, for they have more influence and power than the soldiers. The Grand Turk and the Sultan of Egypt form an exception to this rule, for the Turk always keeps himself surrounded by twelve thousand infantry and fifteen thousand cavalry, on which the strength and security of his empire depends; he must therefore keep these troops devoted to himself, regardless of all consideration for the people.

It is much the same with the government of the Sultan of Egypt, which being entirely under the control of the army, it behooves him also, regardless of the people, to keep the soldiery his friends. And here I would remark that the government of the Sultan of Egypt differs from all other principalities, although in some respects similar to the Christian Pontificate, which cannot be called either an hereditary or a new principality. For when the Sultan dies, his sons do not inherit the government, but it devolves upon whoever is elected to that dignity by those who have authority in the matter. And as this system is consecrated by time, it cannot be called a new principality; for it is free from all the difficulties that appertain to new principalities. For even if the prince be new, the institutions of the state are old, and are so organized as to receive the elected the same as though he were their hereditary lord.

But to return to our subject, I say, that whoever reflects carefully upon the above discourse will find that the ruin of the above-mentioned Emperors was caused by either hatred or contempt; and he will also see how it happened that, while some of them having proceeded one way and some in the opposite, in some instances the one had a happy, and the other an unhappy end. For in the case of Pertinax and Alexander, both being new princes, it was useless and dangerous for them to attempt to imitate Marcus, who had inherited the Empire. And in the same way it was ruinous for Caracalla, Commodus, and Maximinius to imitate Severus, for neither of them possessed the noble qualities necessary to enable them to follow in his footsteps.

A prince, therefore, who has but recently acquired his principality, cannot imitate the conduct of Marcus Aurelius; nor is it necessary for him to imitate that of Septimus Severus. But he should learn from Severus what is necessary to found a state, and from Marcus what is proper and glorious for the preservation of a state that is already firmly established.

CHAPTER XX

*WHETHER THE ERECTION OF FORTRESSES,
AND MANY OTHER THINGS WHICH PRINCES
OFTEN DO, ARE USEFUL OR INJURIOUS*

Some princes, with a view to a more secure tenure of their states, have disarmed their subjects; some have kept the countries subject to them divided into different parties; others have purposely encouraged enmities against themselves; while others again have endeavored to win the good will of those whom in the beginning of their reign they suspected of hostile feelings. Some have built fortresses, while others have demolished and razed those that existed. Now although I cannot pronounce any definite judgment as to these different ways of proceeding, without examining the particular condition of those states where similar proceedings are to be applied, yet I will treat the subject in that general way of which it is susceptible.

It has never happened that a new prince has disarmed his subjects; on the contrary rather, if he has found them unarmed, he has armed them, and in that way has made them as it were his own, and made those faithful who before were suspect; while those who were loyal to him before will remain so, and thus he will convert his subjects into his partisans and supporters. And although a prince cannot arm all his subjects, yet by giving certain advantages to those whom he does arm, he secures himself the better against the others who are not armed, and who will excuse the preference shown to those whom the prince has armed and thereby laid under obligations to himself. For the others will excuse him, and will recognize the necessity of rewarding those who are exposed to greater danger, and who have more onerous duties to perform.

But a prince who disarms his subjects will at once offend them, by thus showing that he has no confidence in them, but that he suspects them either of cowardice or want of loyalty, and this will cause them to hate him. And as the prince cannot remain without an armed force, he will have to resort to mercenaries, the objections to which I have fully set forth in a preceding chapter. And even if these mercenaries were not absolutely bad, they would still be insufficient to protect the prince against powerful enemies, and suspected subjects. Therefore, as I have said, new princes should always establish armed forces in their newly acquired principalities; for which history furnishes us abundance of precedents.

But when a prince acquires a new state, which he annexes as an appendage to his old possessions, then it is advisable for him to disarm the inhabitants of the new state, excepting those who, upon the acquisition of the same, declared in the prince's favor. But even these it will be well for him to weaken and enervate when occasion offers; so that his armed forces shall be organized in such a way as to consist entirely of his own subjects, natives of his original state.

Our ancestors, and those who were regarded as wise, used to say that the way to hold Pistoia was through party divisions, and Pisa by means of fortresses. Accordingly they encouraged such party divisions in some of the towns that were subject to them, for the purpose of holding them the more easily. This may have been very well in those times when the different powers of Italy were to some extent evenly balanced; but it does not seem to me that such a precept is applicable at the present day, for I do not believe that party divisions purposely made are ever productive of good. To the contrary rather, cities divided against themselves are easily lost, on the approach of an enemy; for the weaker party will always unite with the external foe, and then the other will not be able to maintain itself.

The Venetians, influenced I believe by the above reasons, encouraged the feuds between the Guelphs and the Ghibellines in the cities that were subject to them; and although they never allowed them to come to bloody conflicts, yet they fomented their quarrels sufficiently to keep the citizens occupied with their own dissensions, so that they could not turn against the Venetians. This, however, did not result as they had designed, for after the defeat at Vaila one of the parties promptly took courage, and deprived the Venetians of the entire state. Measures of this kind, therefore, argue weakness in a prince, for a strong government will never allow such divisions; they can be of advantage only in time of peace, as by their means subjects may be more easily managed, but in case of war the fallacy of this system becomes manifest. Princes undoubtedly become great by overcoming all difficulties and oppositions that may spring up against them; and therefore does Fortune, when she intends to make a new prince great (for whom it is more important to acquire a reputation than for an hereditary prince), cause enemies to arise and make attempts against the prince, so as to afford him the opportunity of overcoming them, and that he may thus rise higher by means of the very ladder which his enemies have brought against him. And therefore the opinion has been held by many, that a wise prince should, when opportunity offers, adroitly nurse some enmities against himself, so that by overcoming them his greatness may be increased.

Princes, and more especially new ones, have often met with more fidelity and devotion in the very men whom at the beginning of their reign they mistrusted, than in those upon whom they at first confidently relied. Thus Pandolfo Petrucci, Prince of Siena, governed his state more by the aid of those whom he at first regarded with suspicion, than by that of any of his other subjects. But no general rules can be laid down for this, as the prince must in this respect be governed by circumstances. I will only observe that those men who at the beginning of a prince's reign are hostile to him, and who are yet so situated that they need his support for their maintenance, will always be most easily won over by him; and they will be obliged to continue to serve him with the greater fidelity, because of the importance of their effacing by their good conduct the bad opinion which the prince had formed of them at the beginning. And thus the prince will derive more useful service from these than from such as from over confidence in their security will serve his interests negligently.

And since the subject requires it, I will not omit to remind the prince who has but recently acquired a state by the favor of its citizens to consider well the reasons that influenced those who favored his success. For if it was not a natural affection for him, but merely their dissatisfaction with the previous government, then he will have much trouble and difficulty in preserving their attachment, for it will be almost impossible for the prince to satisfy their expectations. Now if we carefully study the reasons of this from the examples which both ancient and modern history furnish us, we shall find that it is much easier for a prince to win the friendship of those who previous to his acquisition of the state were content with its government, and who must therefore have been hostile to him, than of those who, from being malcontents under the previous government, became his friends, and favored his seizing the state.

It has been the general practice of princes, for the purpose of holding their states securely, to build fortresses to serve as a curb and check upon those who might make an attempt against the government, and at the same time to afford the prince a secure place of refuge against the first attack. I approve of this system, because it was practiced by the ancients; and yet we have seen in our own times that Messer Niccolò Vitelli dismantled two fortresses in Città di Castello, so as to enable him to hold that place. Guidobaldo, Duke of Urbino, on returning to his state, whence he had been driven by Cesare Borgia, razed all the fortresses of that province to their very foundations; for he thought that it would be more difficult for him to lose that state a second time without those fortresses. The Bentivogli did the same thing on their return to Bologna. Fortresses then are useful or not, according to circumstances; and while in one way they are advantageous, they may in another prove injurious to a prince. The question may therefore be stated thus. A prince who fears his own people more than he does foreigners should build fortresses; but he who has more cause to fear strangers than his own people should do without them. The citadel of

Milan, built by Francesco Sforza, has caused, and will yet cause, more trouble to the house of Sforza than any other disturbance in that state. The best fortress which a prince can possess is the affection of his people; for even if he have fortresses, and is hated by his people, the fortresses will not save him; for when a people have once risen in arms against their prince, there will be no lack of strangers who will aid them.

In our own times we have seen but one instance where fortresses have been of advantage to a ruler, and that was the case of the Countess of Furli, when her husband, the Count Girolamo, was killed; for the castle of Furli enabled her to escape from the fury of the people, and there to await assistance from Milan, so as to recover her state, the circumstances at the time being such that the people could not obtain assistance from strangers. Later, however, when she was assailed by Cesare Borgia, the people of Furli, being hostile to her, united with the stranger, and then the castle was no longer of any great value to her. Thus she would have been more secure if she had not been hated by her people, than she was in possessing the castle.

After a full examination of the question, then, I approve of those who build fortresses, as well as those who do not. But I blame all those who, in their confident reliance upon such strongholds, do not mind incurring the hatred of their own people.

CHAPTER XXI

HOW PRINCES SHOULD CONDUCT THEM-
SELVES TO ACQUIRE A REPUTATION

Nothing makes a prince so much esteemed as the undertaking of great enterprises and the setting a noble example
in his own person. We have a striking instance of this in
Ferdinand of Aragon, the present King of Spain. He may
be called, as it were, a new prince; for, from being King
of a feeble state, he has, by his fame and glory, become
the first sovereign of Christendom; and if we examine his
actions we shall find them all most grand, and some of
them extraordinary. In the beginning of his reign he attacked Granada, and it was this undertaking that was the
very foundation of his greatness. At first he carried on this
war leisurely and without fear of opposition; for he kept
the nobles of Castile occupied with this enterprise, and,
their minds being thus engaged by war, they gave no attention to the innovations introduced by the King, who
thereby acquired a reputation and an influence over the
nobles without their being aware of it. The money of the
Church and of the people enabled him to support his
armies, and by that long war he succeeded in giving a
stable foundation to his military establishment, which afterward brought him so much honor. Besides this, to be
able to engage in still greater enterprises, he always availed
himself of religion as a pretext, and committed a pious

cruelty in spoliating and driving the Moors out of his kingdom, which certainly was a most admirable and extraordinary example. Under the same cloak of religion he attacked Africa, and made a descent upon Italy, and finally assailed France. And thus he was always planning great enterprises, which kept the minds of his subjects in a state of suspense and admiration, and occupied with their results. And these different enterprises followed so quickly one upon the other, that he never gave men a chance deliberately to make any attempt against himself.

It is also important for a prince to give striking examples of his interior administration (similar to those that are related of Messer Bernabo di Milano) when an occasion presents itself to reward or punish any one who has in civil affairs either rendered great service to the state, or committed some crime, so that it may be much talked about. But, above all, a prince should endeavor to invest all his actions with a character of grandeur and excellence. A prince, furthermore, becomes esteemed when he shows himself either a true friend or a real enemy; that is, when, regardless of consequences, he declares himself openly for or against another, which will always be more creditable to him than to remain neutral. For if two of your neighboring potentates should come to war among themselves, they are either of such character that, when either of them has been defeated, you will have cause to fear the conqueror, or not. In either case, it will always be better for you to declare yourself openly and make fair war; for if you fail to do so, you will be very apt to fall a prey to the victor, to the delight and satisfaction of the defeated party, and you will have no claim for protection or assistance from either the one or the other. For the conqueror will want no doubtful friends, who did not stand by him in time of trial; and the defeated party will not forgive you for having refused, with arms in hand, to take the chance of his fortunes.

When Antiochus came into Greece, having been sent by the Ætolians to drive out the Romans, he sent ambassadors to the Achaians, who were friends of the Romans, to induce them to remain neutral; while the Romans, on the other hand, urged them to take up arms in their behalf. When the matter came up for deliberation in the council of the Achaians, and the ambassadors of Antiochus endeavored to persuade them to remain neutral, the Roman legate replied: "As to the course which is said to be the best and most advantageous for your state, not to intervene in our war, I can assure you that the very reverse will be the case; for by not intervening you will, without thanks and without credit, remain a prize to the victor."

And it will always be the case that he who is not your friend will request neutrality at your hands, while your friend will ask your armed intervention in his favor. Irresolute princes, for the sake of avoiding immediate danger, adopt most frequently the course of neutrality, and are generally ruined in consequence. But when a prince declares himself boldly in favor of one party, and that party proves victorious, even though the victor be powerful, and you are at his discretion, yet is he bound to you in love and obligation; and men are never so base as to repay these by such flagrant ingratitude as the oppressing you under these circumstances would be.[1]

---

[1] Machiavelli is more pessimistic concerning human gratitude and ambition in the first *Discourse*.

Moreover, victories are never so complete as to dispense the victor from all regard for justice. But when the party whom you have supported loses, then he will ever after receive you as a friend, and, when able, will assist you in turn; and thus you will have become the sharer of a fortune which in time may be retrieved.

In the second case, when the contending parties are such that you need not fear the victor, then it is the more prudent to give him your support; for you thereby aid one to ruin the other, whom he should save if he were wise; for although he has defeated his adversary, yet he remains at your discretion, inasmuch as without your assistance victory would have been impossible for him. And here it should be noted, that a prince ought carefully to avoid making common cause with any one more powerful than himself, for the purpose of attacking another power, unless he should be compelled to do so by necessity. For if the former is victorious, then you are at his mercy; and princes should, if possible, avoid placing themselves in such a position.

The Venetians allied themselves with France against the Duke of Milan, an alliance which they could easily have avoided, and which proved their ruin. But when it is unavoidable, as was the case with the Florentines when Spain and the Pope united their forces to attack Lombardy, then a prince ought to join the stronger party, for the reasons above given. Nor is it to be supposed that a state can ever adopt a course that is entirely safe; on the contrary, a prince must make up his mind to take the chance of all the doubts and uncertainties; for such is the order of things that one inconvenience cannot be avoided except at the risk of being exposed to another. And it is the province of prudence to discriminate among these inconveniences, and to accept the least evil for good.

A prince should also show himself a lover of virtue, and should honor all who excel in any one of the arts, and should encourage his citizens quietly to pursue their vocations, whether of commerce, agriculture, or any other human industry; so that the one may not abstain from embellishing his possessions for fear of their being taken from him, nor the other from opening new sources of commerce for fear of taxes. But the prince should provide rewards for those who are willing to do these things, and for all who strive to enlarge his city or state. And besides this, he should at suitable periods amuse his people with festivities and spectacles. And as cities are generally divided into guilds and classes, he should keep account of these bodies, and occasionally be present at their assemblies, and should set an example of his affability and magnificence; preserving, however, always the majesty of his dignity, which should never be wanting on any occasion or under any circumstances.

CHAPTER XXII

OF THE MINISTERS OF PRINCES

The choice of his ministers is of no slight importance to a prince; they are either good or not, according as the prince himself is sagacious or otherwise; and upon the character of the persons with whom a prince surrounds himself depends the first impression that is formed of his own ability. If his ministers and counselors are competent and faithful, he will be reputed wise, because he had known how to discern their capacity and how to secure their fidelity; but if they prove otherwise, then the opinion formed of the prince will not be favorable, because of his want of judgment in their first selection. Every one who knew Messer Antonio di Venafro as the minister of Pandolfo Petrucci, Prince of Siena, judged Pandolfo to be a man of great sagacity in having chosen Messer Antonio for his minister.

There are three sorts of intellect: the one understands things by its own quickness of perception; another understands them when explained by some one else; and the third understands them neither by itself nor by the explanation of others. The first is the best, the second very good, and the third useless. Now we must admit that Pandolfo did not belong to the first order, but rather to the second. For whenever a prince has the sagacity to recognize the good or the evil that is said or done, he will, even without being a genius, be able to judge whether the minister's actions are good or bad; and he will praise the one and censure the other. And thus the minister, seeing that he cannot hope to deceive the prince, will continue to serve him faithfully. But the true way for a prince to know his minister is as follows, and never fails. Whenever he sees that the minister thinks more of himself than of the prince, and that in all his doings he seeks his own advantage more than that of the state, then the prince may be sure that that man will never be a good minister, and is not to be trusted. For a man who has the administration of a state in his hands, should never think of himself, but only of the prince, and should never bring anything to his notice that does not relate to the interest of the government.

On the other hand, the prince, by way of securing the devotion of his minister, should think of him and bind him to himself by obligations; he should bestow riches upon him, and should share the honors as well as the cares with him; so that the abundance of honors and riches conferred by the prince upon his minister may cause the latter not to desire either the one or the other from any other source, and that the weight of cares may make him dread a change, knowing that without the prince he could not sustain it. And when the relations between the prince and his minister are thus constituted, they will be able to confide in each other; but if they be otherwise, then one or the other of them will surely come to a bad end.

CHAPTER XXIII

HOW TO AVOID FLATTERERS

I will not leave unnoticed an important subject, and an evil against which princes have much difficulty in defending themselves, if they are not extremely prudent, or have not made good choice of ministers; and this relates to flatterers, who abound in all courts. Men are generally so well pleased with themselves and their own acts, and delude themselves to such a degree, that it is with difficulty they escape from the pest of flatterers; and in their efforts to avoid them they expose themselves to the risk of being scorned. There is no other way of guarding against adulation, than to make people understand that they will not offend you by speaking the truth. On the other hand, when every one feels at liberty to tell you the truth, they will be apt to be lacking in respect to you. A prudent prince therefore should follow a middle course, choosing for ministers of his government only wise men, and to these only should he give full power to tell him the truth, and they should only be allowed to speak to him of those things which he asks of them, and of none other. But then the prince should ask them about everything, and should listen to their opinions and reflect upon them, and afterward form his own resolutions. And he should bear himself toward all his advisers in such manner that each may know that the more freely he speaks, the more acceptable will he be. But outside of these he should not listen to any one, but follow the course agreed upon, and be firm in his resolves. Whoever acts otherwise will either be misled by his flatterers, or will vacillate in his decisions, because of the variety of opinions; and this will naturally result in his losing in public estimation.

I will cite one modern example to this effect. Padre Luca, in the service of the present Emperor Maximilian, in speaking of his Majesty, says that he "counsels with no one, and yet never does anything in his own way"; which results from his following the very opposite course to that above indicated; for the Emperor is a reserved man, who never communicates his secrets to any one, nor takes advice from anybody. But when he attempts to carry his plans into execution and they begin to be known, then also do they begin to be opposed by those whom he has around him; and being easily influenced, he is diverted from his own resolves. And thence it comes that he undoes one day what he has done the day before, and that one never knows what he wants or designs to do; and therefore his conclusions cannot be depended upon.

A prince nevertheless should always take counsel, but only when he wants it, and not when others wish to thrust it upon him; in fact, he should rather discourage persons from tendering him advice unsolicited by him. But he should be an extensive questioner, and a patient listener to the truth respecting the things inquired about, and should even show his anger in case any one should, for some reason, not tell him the truth.

Those who imagine that a prince who has the reputation of sagacity is not indebted for it to his own natural gifts, but to the good counsels of those who surround him, certainly deceive themselves. For it may be taken as a general and infallible rule, that a prince who is not naturally wise cannot be well advised; unless he should perchance place himself entirely in the hands of one man, who should guide him in all things, and who would have to be a man of uncommon ability. In such a case a prince might be well directed, but it would probably not last long, because his counselor would in a short time deprive him of his state. But a prince who is not wise himself, and counsels with more than one person, will never have united counsels; for he will himself lack the ability to harmonize and combine the various counsels and suggestions. His advisers will only think of their own advantage, which the prince will neither know how to discern nor how to correct.

And things cannot well be otherwise, for men will always naturally prove bad, unless some necessity constrains them to be good. Whence we conclude that good counsels, no matter whence they may come, result wholly from the prince's own sagacity; but the wisdom of the prince never results from good counsels.

CHAPTER XXIV

THE REASON WHY THE PRINCES OF ITALY HAVE LOST THEIR STATES

A judicious observation of the above-given rules will cause a new prince to be regarded as though he were an hereditary one, and will very soon make him more firm and secure in his state than if he had grown old in its possession. For the actions of a new prince are much more closely observed and scrutinized than those of an hereditary one; and when they are known to be virtuous, they will win the confidence and affections of men much more for the new prince, and make his subjects feel under greater obligations to him, than if he were of the ancient line. For men are ever more taken with the things of the present than with those of the past; and when they find their own good in the present, then they enjoy it and seek none other, and will be ready in every way to defend the new prince, provided he be not wanting to himself in other respects. And thus he will have the double glory of having established a new principality, and of having strengthened and adorned it with good laws, good armies, good allies, and good examples. And in the same way will it be a double shame to an hereditary prince, if through want of prudence and ability he loses his state.

If now we examine the conduct of those princes of Italy who in our day have lost their states, such as the King of Naples, the Duke of Milan, and others, we shall note in them at once a common defect as regards their military forces, for the reasons which we have discussed at length above. And we shall also find that in some instances the people were hostile to the prince; or if he had the good will of the people, he knew not how to conciliate that of the nobles. For unless there be some such defects as these, states are not lost when the prince has energy enough to keep an army in the field.

Philip of Macedon, not the father of Alexander the Great, but he who was vanquished by Titus Quintus, had not much of a state as compared with Rome and Greece, who attacked him; yet being a military man, and at the same time knowing how to preserve the good will of the people and to assure himself of the support of the nobles, he sustained the war against the Romans and Greeks for many years; and although he finally lost some cities, yet he preserved his kingdom.

Those of our princes, therefore, who have lost their dominions after having been established in them for many years, should not blame fortune, but only their own indolence and lack of energy; for in times of quiet they never thought of the possibility of a change (it being a common defect of men in fair weather to take no thought of storms), and afterward, when adversity overtook them, their first impulse was to fly, and not to defend themselves, hoping that the people, when disgusted with the insolence of the victors, would recall them. Such a course may be very well when others fail, but it is very discreditable to neglect other means for it that might have saved you from ruin; for no one ever falls deliberately, in the expectation that some one will help him up, which either does not happen, or, if it does, will not contribute to your security; for it is a base thing to look to others for your defense instead of depending upon yourself. That defense alone is effectual, sure, and durable which depends upon yourself and your own valor.

CHAPTER XXV

OF THE INFLUENCE OF FORTUNE IN HUMAN AFFAIRS, AND HOW IT MAY BE COUNTERACTED

I am well aware that many have held and still hold the opinion, that the affairs of this world are so controlled by Fortune and by the Divine Power that human wisdom and foresight cannot modify them; that, in fact, there is no remedy against the decrees of fate, and that therefore it is not worth while to make any effort, but to yield unconditionally to the power of Fortune. This opinion has been generally accepted in our times, because of the great changes that have taken place, and are still being witnessed every day, and are beyond all human conjecture.

In reflecting upon this at times, I am myself in some measure inclined to that belief; nevertheless, as our free will is not entirely destroyed, I judge that it may be assumed as true that Fortune to the extent of one half is the arbiter of our actions, but that she permits us to direct the other half, or perhaps a little less, ourselves. I compare this to a swollen river, which in its fury overflows the plains, tears up the trees and buildings, and sweeps the earth from one place and deposits it in another. Every one flies before the flood, and yields to its fury, unable to resist it; and notwithstanding this state of things, men do not when the river is in its ordinary condition provide against its overflow by dikes and walls, so that when it rises it may flow either in the channel thus provided for it, or that at any rate its violence may not be entirely unchecked, nor its effects prove so injurious. It is the same with Fortune, who displays her power where there is no organized valor to resist her, and where she knows that there are no dikes or walls to control her.

If now you examine Italy, which is the seat of the changes under consideration, and has occasioned their occurrence, you will see that she is like an open country, without dikes or any other protection against inundations; and that if she had been protected with proper valor and wisdom, as is the case with Germany, Spain, and France, these inundations would either not have caused the great changes which they did, or they would not have occurred at all.

These remarks I deem sufficient as regards resisting fortune in general; but confining myself now more to particular cases, I say that we see a prince fortunate one day, and ruined the next, without his nature or any of his qualities being changed. I believe this results mainly from the causes which have been discussed at length above; namely, that the prince who relies entirely upon fortune will be ruined according as fortune varies. I believe, further, that the prince who conforms his conduct to the spirit of the times will be fortunate; and in the same way will he be unfortunate, if in his actions he disregards the spirit of the times. For we see men proceed in various ways to attain the end they aim at, such as glory and riches: the one with circumspection, the other with rashness; one with violence, another with cunning; one with patience, and another with impetuosity; and all may succeed in their different ways. We also see that, of two men equally prudent, the one will accomplish his designs, while the other fails; and in the same way we see two men succeed equally well by two entirely different methods, the one being prudent and the other rash; which is due to nothing else than the character of the times, to which they either conform in their proceedings or not. Whence it comes, as I have said, that two men by entirely different modes of action will achieve the same results; while of two others, proceeding precisely in the same way, the one will accomplish his end, and the other not. This also causes the difference of success; for if one man, acting with caution and patience, is also favored by time and circumstances, he will be successful; but if these change, then will he be ruined, unless, indeed, he changes his conduct accordingly. Nor is there any man so sagacious that he will always know how to conform to such change of times and circumstances; for men do not readily deviate from the course to which their nature inclines them; and, moreover, if they have generally been prosperous by following one course, they cannot persuade themselves that it would be well to depart from it. Thus the cautious man, when the moment comes for him to strike a bold blow, will not know how to do it, and thence will he fail; while if he could have changed his nature with the times and circumstances, his usual good fortune would not have abandoned him.

Pope Julius II was in all his actions most impetuous; and the times and circumstances happened so to conform to that mode of proceeding that he always achieved happy results. Witness the first attempt he made upon Bologna, when Messer Giovanni Bentivogli was still living. This attempt gave umbrage to the Venetians, and also to the kings of Spain and France, who held a conference on the subject. But Pope Julius, with his habitual boldness and impetuosity, assumed the direction of that expedition in person; which caused the Spaniards and the Venetians to remain quiet in suspense, the latter from fear, and the others from a desire to recover the entire kingdom of Naples. On the other hand, the Pope drew the King of France after him; for that King, seeing that Julius had already started on the expedition, and wishing to gain his friendship for the purpose of humbling the Venetians, judged that he could not refuse him the assistance of his army without manifest injury to himself.

Pope Julius II, then, achieved by this impetuous movement what no other pontiff could have accomplished with all possible human prudence. For had he waited to start from Rome until all his plans were definitely arranged, and everything carefully organized, as every other pontiff would have done, he would certainly never have succeeded; for the King would have found a thousand excuses, and the others would have caused him a thousand apprehensions. I will not dwell upon the other actions of Julius II, which were all of a similar character, and have all succeeded equally well. The shortness of his life saved him from experiencing any reverses; for if times had supervened that would have made it necessary for him to proceed with caution and prudence, he would assuredly have been ruined; for he could never have deviated from the course to which his nature inclined him.

I conclude, then, inasmuch as Fortune is changeable, that men who persist obstinately in their own ways will be successful only so long as those ways coincide with those of Fortune; and whenever these differ, they fail. But, on the whole, I judge impetuosity to be better than caution; for Fortune is a woman, and if you wish to master her, you must strike and beat her, and you will see that she allows herself to be more easily vanquished by the rash and the violent than by those who proceed more slowly and coldly. And therefore, as a woman, she ever favors youth more than age, for youth is less cautious and more energetic, and commands Fortune with greater audacity.

CHAPTER XXVI

EXHORTATION TO DELIVER ITALY FROM FOREIGN BARBARIANS

Reviewing now all I have said in the foregoing discourses, and thinking to myself that, if the present time should be favorable for Italy to receive and honor a new prince, and the opportunity were given to a prudent and virtuous man to establish a new form of government, that would bring honor to himself and happiness to the mass of the Italian people, so many things would combine for the advantage of such a new prince, that, so far as I know, no previous time was ever more favorable for such a change. And if, as I have said, it was necessary for the purpose of displaying the virtue of Moses that the people of Israel should be held in bondage in Egypt; and that the Persians should be opposed to the Medes, so as to bring to light the greatness and courage of Cyrus; and that the Athenians should be dispersed for the purpose of illustrating the excellence of Theseus; so at present, for the purpose of making manifest the virtues of one Italian spirit, it was necessary that Italy should have been brought to her present condition of being in a worse bondage than that of the Jews, more enslaved than the Persians, more scattered than the Athenians, without a head, without order, vanquished and despoiled, lacerated, overrun by her enemies, and subjected to every kind of devastation.

And although, up to the present time, there may have been some one who may have given a gleam of hope that he was ordained by Heaven to redeem Italy, yet have we seen how, in the very zenith of his career, he was so checked by fortune that poor Italy remained as it were lifeless, and waiting to see who might be chosen to heal her wounds,—to put an end to her devastation, to the sacking of Lombardy, to the spoliation and ruinous taxation of the kingdom of Naples and of Tuscany—and who should heal her sores that have festered so long. You see how she prays God that he may send some one who shall redeem her from this cruelty and barbarous insolence. You see her eagerly disposed to follow any banner, provided there be some one to bear it aloft. But there is no one at present in whom she could place more hope than in your illustrious house, O magnificent Lorenzo! which, with its virtue and fortune, favored by God and the Church, of which it is now the head, could make an effectual beginning of her deliverance. And this will not be difficult for you, if you will first study carefully the lives and actions of the men whom I have named above. And although these men were rare and wonderful, they were

115

nevertheless but men, and the opportunities which they had were far less favorable than the present; nor were their undertakings more just or more easy than this; neither were they more favored by the Almighty than what you are. Here, then, is great justice; for war is just when it is necessary, and a resort to arms is beneficent when there is no hope in anything else. The opportunity is most favorable, and when that is the case there can be no great difficulties, provided you follow the course of those whom I have held up to you as examples. Although in their case extraordinary things, without parallel, were brought about by the hand of God,—the sea divided for their passage, a pillar of cloud pointed their way through the wilderness, the rock poured forth water to assuage their thirst, and it rained manna to appease their hunger,—yet your greatness combines all, and on your own efforts will depend the result. God will not do everything; for that would deprive us of our free will, and of that share of glory which belongs to us.

Nor should we wonder that not one of the Italians whom I have mentioned has been able to accomplish that which it is to be hoped will be done by your illustrious house; for if in so many revolutions in Italy, and in the conduct of so many wars, it would seem that military capacity and valor have become extinct, it is owing to the fact that the old military system was defective, and no one has come forward capable of establishing a new one. And nothing brings a man who has newly risen so much honor as the establishing of new laws and institutions of his own creation; if they have greatness in them and become well established, they will make the prince admired and revered; and there is no lack of opportunity in Italy for the introduction of every kind of reform. The people have great courage, provided it be not wanting in their leaders. Look but at their single combats, and their encounters when there are but a few on either side, and see how superior the Italians have shown themselves in strength, dexterity, and ability. But when it comes to their armies, then these qualities do not appear, because of the incapacity of the chiefs, who cannot enforce obedience from those who are versed in the art of war, and every one believes himself to be so; for up to the present time there have been none so decidedly superior in valor and good fortune that the others yielded him obedience. Thence it comes that in so great a length of time, and in the many wars that have occurred within the past twenty years, the armies, whenever wholly composed of Italians, have given but poor account of themselves. Witness first Taro, then Alessandria, Capua, Genoa, Vaila, Bologna, and Mestri.

If, then, your illustrious house is willing to follow the examples of those distinguished men who have redeemed their countries, you will before anything else, and as the very foundation of every enterprise, have to provide yourself with a national army. And you cannot have more faithful, truer, and better soldiers than the Italians. And while each individual is good, they will become still better when they are all united, and know that they are commanded by their own prince, who will honor and support them. It is necessary, therefore, to provide troops of this kind, so as to be able successfully to oppose Italian valor to the attacks of foreigners.

And although the infantry of the Swiss and of the Spaniards is looked upon as terrible, yet both of them have a defect, which will permit a third organization not only to resist them, but confidently hope to vanquish them. For the Spaniards cannot withstand the shock of cavalry, and the Swiss dread infantry, when they encounter it in battle as obstinate as themselves. Whence we have seen, what further experience will prove more fully, that the Spaniards cannot resist the French cavalry, and that the Swiss succumb to the Spanish infantry. And although we have not yet had a full trial of the latter, yet have we had a fair specimen of it in the battle of Ravenna, where the Spanish infantry confronted the line of battle of the Germans, who have adopted the same system as the Swiss; and where the Spaniards with great agility, and protected by their bucklers, rushed under the pikes of the Germans, and were thus able to attack them securely without the Germans being able to prevent it; and had it not been for the cavalry which fell upon the Spaniards, they might have destroyed the entire German infantry.

Knowing, then, the defects of the one and the other of these systems of infantry, you can organize a new one that shall avoid these defects, and shall be able to resist cavalry as well as infantry. And this is to be done, not by a change of arms, but by an entirely different organization and discipline. This is one of the things which, if successfully introduced, will give fame and greatness to a new prince.

You must not, then, allow this opportunity to pass, so that Italy, after waiting so long, may at last see her deliverer appear. Nor can I possibly express with what affection he would be received in all those provinces that have suffered so long from this inundation of foreign foes!— with what thirst for vengeance, with what persistent faith, with what devotion, and with what tears! What door would be closed to him? Who would refuse him obedience? What envy would dare oppose him? What Italian would refuse him homage? This barbarous dominion of the foreigner offends the very nostrils of everybody!

Let your illustrious house, then, assume this task with that courage and hopefulness which every just enterprise inspires; so that under your banner our country may recover its ancient fame, and under your auspices may be verified the words of Petrarca:—

"Virtù contro al furore
  Prenderà l' arme, e fia il combatter corto;
Chè l' antico valore
  Negli Italici cuor non è ancor morto."

  —Canz. XVI, v. 93-96.[1]

---

[1] Courage will take up arms against the barbarian, and may the struggle be brief; for the valor of old is not yet extinguished in Italian hearts.